Windows™ 3.1 Quick Reference

Que Quick Reference Series

TIMOTHY S. STANLEY

D1125630

que

Windows 3.1 Quick Reference.

Copyright© 1992 by Que® Corporation.

Library of Congress Catalog Number: 91-61974

ISBN: 0-88022-740-0

95 94   10 9

Interpretation of the printing code: the rightmost double-digit number is the year of the book's printing; the rightmost single-digit number is the number of the book's printing. For example, a printing code of 92-4 shows that the fourth printing of the book occurred in 1992.

This book is based on Windows 3.1.

CREDITS

Publisher
Lloyd J. Short

Production Editor
Pamela D. Wampler

Technical Editor
Gary J. Pickavet

Production Team
Mark Enochs, Brook Farling, Carrie Keesling,
Betty Kish, Bob LaRoche, Laurie Lee, Jay
Lesandrini, Susan VandeWalle, Phil Worthington

TRADEMARK ACKNOWLEDGMENTS

TABLE OF CONTENTS

INTRODUCTION

Windows 3.1 Quick Reference not only includes the quick reference information you need to manage applications, but reviews the various commands and options available with Windows 3.1. You learn to perform many tasks that are necessary to operate Windows successfully.

Because it is a quick reference, this book is not intended to replace the extensive documentation included with Windows 3.1. For further information, supplement this book with Que's *Using Windows 3.1*, Special Edition.

This Quick Reference highlights the most frequently used information and reference material required to work quickly and efficiently with Windows. For example, the documentation includes pages of information on how to use the File Manager. *Windows 3.1 Quick Reference* does not repeat that extensive documentation. Instead, this book provides step-by-step instructions on how to perform many of the tasks involved in using the File Manager.

This book is divided into sections by tasks. One task, for example, is called "Copy Files." This section provides the step-by-step instructions needed to copy files using the File Manager.

Now you can put essential information at your fingertips with *Windows 3.1 Quick Reference*—and the entire Que Quick Reference series.

Windows Applications

Windows 3.1 is a multitasking operating environment for MS-DOS. It is called an "environment" because programs are designed to work in and take advantage of Windows. Windows manages the applications that are designed for it, giving all programs a similar, consistent look and feel, and Windows enables you to operate more than one program at a time. Although you may have Windows so that you can use powerful programs such as Excel, Word for Windows, and PageMaker, you should not overlook the following accessories that accompany Windows:

Accessory	Description
Notepad	A simple text editor used to record reminder notes, or to create and modify ASCII files, such as batch files.
Recorder	A program that creates macros of repetitious keystrokes and mouse movements.
Cardfile	A card-type database (such as a Rolodex).
Calendar	An appointment scheduler with an alarm.
Calculator	A desktop calculator with scientific and financial functions.

Accessory	Description
Clock	An on-screen analog or digital clock.
PIF Editor	A program for creating Program Information Files enabling DOS applications to run in the Windows environment.
File Manager	A shell to manage directories and files.
Clipboard	An area of memory that holds text or graphics you want transferred between programs.
Control Panel	A program that enables you to customize Windows.
Print Manager	A program that enables Windows to manage and spool print jobs.
Windows Setup	A program that enables you to change Windows system settings, add applications, create PIFs automatically, and add or remove Windows components.
Paintbrush	A bit-map drawing program that supports colors.
Terminal	A communications program.
Write	A simple word processor.
Character Map	A program that lets you select characters not easily accessible on the keyboard.

continues

Accessory	Description
Object Packager	A program that enables you to store any information as an icon for inclusion in a program.
Media Player	A program that enables you to control multimedia devices.
Sound Recorder	A program that enables you to record, modify, and mix sounds.
Solitaire	The game of solitaire.
Minesweeper	A game of memory.

Hints for Using This Book

Because Windows 3.1 consists of many different areas, this Quick Reference includes a subhead under each boxed header. The subhead refers you to a specific Windows 3.1 area. The subhead tells you which program to run to achieve the desired result. For example, the subhead "File Manager" under the heading "Selecting Files" tells you that the commands you need to execute are located in the File Manager.

Conventions used in this book

As you use this book, you need to know a few terms and techniques. Most instructions provide two ways to access the menu: using the keyboard and using the mouse.

The following is a keyboard instruction:

Press Alt+O.

To perform the action, press and hold down the Alt key, press the O key, and then release both keys.

Here is another instruction:

Select the File menu.

To select the menu with the mouse, move the mouse until the mouse pointer is on the menu name. Then click the mouse. (To click the mouse, press and release the left mouse button. To double-click the mouse, press and release the left mouse button twice in rapid succession.)

To select the menu with the keyboard, press the key associated with the boldfaced blue letter—the F key. Words that contain boldfaced blue characters indicate menus, menu items, or options you select. Note that the boldfaced letter appears underlined on the Windows screen.

The mouse

When you *click the mouse*, you press the left mouse button once. When you *double-click the mouse*, you press the left mouse button twice in rapid succession.

When you *point with the mouse*, you move the mouse so that the tip of the on-screen arrow (the mouse pointer) is covering the object you are pointing to. Generally, you point to an object before you select or choose it.

When you *drag an object*, you point to the object with the mouse pointer, hold down the left mouse button, and move the mouse. When the object is in the correct location, release the mouse button.

When you *choose an item*, you make the item active. Sometimes you can choose an item, such as a menu or menu option, by clicking the mouse. Other times, as with Program Item icons or Minimized Application icons, you must double-click the mouse in order to choose the item.

When you *select an item*, you prepare the item to be acted upon. Usually when you select an item, you highlight it. For example, before you copy a file, you highlight the file. To select an item with the mouse, point to the item and click the mouse.

Dialog boxes

A *dialog box* is a box that appears on-screen to give you a message or enable you to select other options. Normally, the dialog box has a title bar that tells you the purpose of the box.

You can select options in a dialog box in different ways. One way is by using an *option button*. An option button is a circle; the center appears solid if the option is selected, or clear if the option is not selected.

You also can select an option by selecting a *check box*; an X appears in the check box if the option is selected.

Dialog boxes also contain *text boxes* (boxes in which you type text), *list boxes* (boxes that display a list of items you select), and *drop-down list boxes* (boxes that display a list of options when you choose the drop-down arrow).

The Windows Desktop

Notice the sample desktop shown in the figure. Each part of the desktop is labeled with a number. Consult the list that follows the figure for a description of the numbered items.

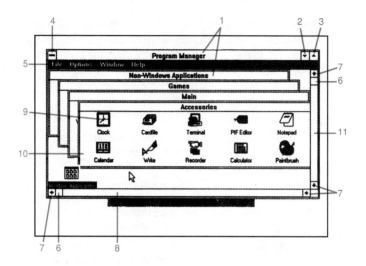

The following is a list of elements that make up the
desktop:

Element	Description
1 Title bar	Tells you the name of the program and data file if applicable, or the name of the dialog box.
2 Minimize button	Reduces the size of the window.
3 Maximize button	Expands the open window.
4 Control menu	Offers the options Restore, Move, Size, Minimize, Maximize, Close, and Switch To.
5 Menu bar	Displays the menu items used to control the application.

continues

Element	Description
6 Scroll box	Displays your file position. Can be "dragged" to move your position in the file.
7 Scroll arrows	Controls the scroll box.
8 Scroll bar	Combines the action of the scroll arrows and scroll box.
9 Icon	A small picture that appears if an application is minimized or hasn't been activated.
10 Window	The entire entity made up of at least a Control menu, title bar, and borders.
11 Window border	The outside frame of the window.

COMMAND REFERENCE

Following is an alphabetical listing of Windows commands and the procedures required to achieve specific results.

386 Enhanced Mode

PIF Editor

Purpose

Creates a Program Information File (PIF) that contains information Windows must know to allocate computer resources for a non-Windows program.

To select the 386 Enhanced mode

1. Start the PIF Editor from the Main program group.

2. Select the Mode menu.

   A check mark appears next to the currently selected mode.

3. If the check mark does not appear next to 386 Enhanced, then select 386 Enhanced.

To enter information for the 386 Enhanced mode (using Lotus 1-2-3 Release 2.2 as an example)

1. Select **P**rogram Filename.

   Enter the entire file name to start the program within the box. Include the path, root name, and extension. In this example, type

   C:\123\LOTUS.COM.

2. Select Window **T**itle.

   Enter the name that appears at the top of the window. For example, type Lotus Access System.

3. Select **O**ptional Parameters. These parameters, such as switches, are used when the program starts.

   Lotus 1-2-3 enables you to supply a different configuration, called a SET file. For example, you can type COLOR.SET, if it is the name of a valid configuration file.

4. Select **S**tart-up Directory.

   Enter the directory name the program will use. Some programs store their data in the current directory. In this example, type C:\123.

5. Select the **V**ideo Memory display option. Select Text if the application only displays text. Choose Low Graphics or High Graphics if the application displays graphics. Text requires less memory than High Graphics. Use the arrow keys or click the option button.

6. Enter the memory required to run the program in the KB **R**equired field. For example, if the minimum memory required to run the program is 256K, then type 256. Specify -1 to allocate as much memory as possible.

7. Enter the memory desired to run the program in the KB **D**esired field. For example, if the

memory desired to run the program is 640K, then type 640. Specify -1 to allocate as much memory as possible.

8. Enter the minimum amount of EMS Memory (expanded memory) the application requires in the KB Required field. Enter an exact number or 0 if no EMS memory is needed.

   If the application requires 350K of EMS memory, for example, then type 350.

9. Enter the maximum amount of EMS Memory the application may use in the KB Limit field. Enter -1 if the application may use as much expanded memory as is needed, 0 if the application should not access expanded memory, or an exact number that is equal to or greater than the number you entered for KB Required.

   If 512K is the most expanded memory to which the application can gain access, then enter 512 in the KB Limit field.

10. Enter the minimum amount of XMS Memory (extended memory) the application requires. In the KB Required field, enter 0 if no XMS memory is needed or enter an exact number.

    If the application requires 350K of XMS memory, then type 350.

11. Enter the maximum amount of XMS Memory the application may use in the KB Limit field. Enter -1 if the application may use as much extended memory as is needed, 0 if the application should not access extended memory, or an exact number that is equal to or greater than the number you entered in the KB Required field.

    If 512K is the most extended memory to which the application can gain access, then type 512.

12. Select how you want the program displayed. Under Display Usage, select Full Screen if you

want the program to use the entire screen, or Windowed if you want the program to run in a window, sharing the screen with other applications.

13. Specify Execution. Select Background if you want the program to continue operating when it is not the foreground program. If you do not select Background, the program will halt when it is switched from the foreground. Select Exclusive if you want the program to have full access to the computer when it is in the foreground and running full-screen. All other programs will halt. If the program is running in a window, then Windows' resources will be minimal, giving maximum resources to the program.

14. Select Close Window on Exit if you want the window to close when you quit the program.

To see the 386 Enhanced mode's Advanced options

1. From the main PIF Editor window, select Advanced.

2. Enter a number from 1 to 10,000 for the Background Priority. The default number is 50.

3. Enter a number from 1 to 10,000 for the Foreground Priority. The default number is 100.

4. Selecting Detect Idle Time enables Windows to see whether the current program is in a waiting condition, such as waiting for keyboard input. If the program is waiting, more computer time will be allocated to a background task.

5. Select EMS Memory Locked if the application using EMS memory should not be swapped to disk. The application then will be locked into memory.

6. Select XMS Memory Locked to keep the application in memory only, which does not allow the application to be swapped to disk.

7. Select High Memory Area to enable an application to access the high memory area (HMA). If a program is using the HMA when Windows starts, then another program may not have access to the HMA. However, Windows enables programs to have their own HMA, so select this check box for best results.

8. Select Lock Application Memory to keep Windows from swapping parts of the program to disk to make room for other programs.

9. Select the Monitor Ports display option. Select Text, Low Graphics, or High Graphics, depending on how the software is installed. To select an option, use the arrow keys and space bar, or click the option.

10. Select Emulate Text Mode to make a text-only application refresh the screen quicker.

    If the screen becomes garbled while Emulate Text Mode is selected, then deselect Emulate Text Mode.

11. Select Retain Video Memory to save the screen when you switch from the program.

    When you select this option, the memory is set aside and not given back, even if you change video modes. The memory set aside is freed when you close the application.

12. Select Allow Fast Paste if the application allows text to be pasted into it.

13. Select Allow Close When Active to quit a non-Windows application when you quit Windows.

    Note that closing an application other than with the normal procedure can cause data to be damaged or lost.

14. Select Reserve Shortcut Keys to enable the program to use the key combinations Alt+Tab, Alt+Esc, Ctrl+Esc, PrtSc, Alt+PrtSc, Alt+space bar, or Alt+Enter.

    Select each key combination with the arrow keys and the space bar, or click the option you want.

    Windows then ignores each key combination you select while running that program.

15. Select Application Shortcut Key to use a key combination to make the application the current one.

16. To quit making changes to Advanced Options, press Enter or click OK.

    To abort the Advanced Options, press Esc or click Cancel.

To save the PIF

1. Select the File menu.

2. Select Save As.

3. Select File Name and type the name of the PIF, using no more than eight characters. If necessary, select the desired drive and directory to save the PIF to.

4. Press Enter or click OK to complete the save.

Notes

PIFs for Windows running in Standard mode differ from PIFs for 386 Enhanced mode. A Standard mode PIF contains information on memory requirements, screen type (text or graphics), and whether the program directly communicates with a serial port. If you have a computer based on the 80386 or 80486 microprocessors and operate in 386 Enhanced

mode, however, you can run several DOS applications at once. To multitask applications, Windows
must have more information about each application
than is required to run a single DOS application.

When you select 386 Enhanced mode, you must
specify whether the application can run in a window
or must occupy the entire screen. You also must
specify whether the application can operate in the
background. If you specify that the application
can run in the background, you must allot how
much computer time to give to the background
application.

386 Enhanced Options

Control Panel

Purpose

Enables Windows to better manage a Windows
application (such as Excel) with a non-Windows
application (such as WordPerfect).

To start the following procedures, start the Control
Panel. Then double-click the 386 Enhanced icon, or
press the arrow keys to select the 386 Enhanced
icon and press Enter.

To set 386 Enhanced options

1. From the 386 Enhanced dialog box, choose
   Device Contention by pressing Alt+D or by
   clicking the first device in the Device Contention list box.

2. Choose the device to set up. For example,
   select COM1.

3. Choose either Always Warn, Never Warn, or
   Idle (in sec.) by pressing Alt+A, Alt+N, or Alt+I
   or by clicking the adjacent option button. The
   meanings of the options are as follows:

Always Warn — Displays a message when a program tries to access a port that is already in use. You choose which application has priority over the port. In most instances, choose this option.

Never Warn — Enables any application to use any port at any time without warning. Choosing this option may cause problems. For example, if two applications send information to the printer, your printout may contain information from both applications. In most instances, do not select this option.

Idle (in sec.) — Allows an application access to a port only if the port has not been used for a specified number of seconds. If you select this option, you must specify the number of seconds that a port should set idle.

4. Repeat steps 2 through 3 for additional ports.

5. Choose Windows in Foreground. Type a number from 1 to 10,000. The default setting is 100.

   This option specifies how much computer time a Windows application will have when it is in the foreground and when a non-Windows application is running in the background. The larger the number you enter, the more time you allot the Windows application and the faster it will run.

6. Choose Windows in Background. Type a number from 1 to 10,000. The default setting is 50.

   This option specifies how much computer time a Windows application will have when it is running in the background and a non-Windows application is running in the foreground. The larger the number you enter, the more time you allot the Windows application and the faster it will run.

7. Choose Exclusive in Foreground if you want a Windows application to have all the computer time when it is in the foreground, even though a non-Windows application is running in the background. If you select this option, the foreground Windows application will get 100 percent of the computer time, while the non-Windows application will halt. When the non-Windows application is made the foreground application, it will operate as normal.

8. Select Minimum Timeslice (in msec). Enter the number of milliseconds (thousandths of a second) that an application will have when it receives a timeslice. The default setting is 100.

9. To save the changes, press Enter or click OK.

To set up virtual memory

1. From the 386 Enhanced dialog box, choose the Virtual Memory button by pressing Alt+V or by clicking Virtual Memory. The Virtual Memory dialog box appears.

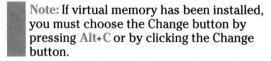

> Note: If virtual memory has been installed, you must choose the Change button by pressing Alt+C or by clicking the Change button.

2. Choose the Drive list box by pressing Alt+D or by clicking the Drive drop-down list arrow.

3. Choose the drive to hold the virtual memory file.

4. Choose the Type list box by pressing Alt+T or by clicking the Type drop-down list arrow.

5. Choose Temporary, Permanent, or None. The meaning of each is as follows:

Temporary	The virtual memory file is created each time Windows starts. When you are not using Windows, the virtual memory file does not exist on the drive.
Permanent	The virtual memory file is created on the drive and remains there, even when Windows is not used. A permanent virtual memory file offers better performance than a Temporary virtual memory file.
None	No virtual memory file is created.

6. Choose the New Size text box by pressing Alt+S or by clicking in the New Size text box.

7. Type a size for the swap file, or accept the default size.

8. Press Enter or click OK to accept the changes. To use the new virtual memory file, you must restart Windows.

Notes

The 386 Enhanced options manage parallel and serial ports by warning you if two applications try to use the same port. These options also manage how much computer time is allotted to each program. Windows slices time, and gives each application a *timeslice*. You may customize each timeslice with 386 Enhanced options.

With an 80386-based or 80486-based computer, Windows can use more memory than your computer actually has by accessing virtual memory. Virtual memory is disk space that is used as RAM. Virtual

memory is slower than RAM; however, virtual
memory prevents out-of-memory errors.

Add/Remove Windows Files

Setup

Purpose

Adds or removes files Windows can use; for
example, adds or deletes bit-mapped images,
accessories, or games that use disk space but are
unnecessary to the operation of Windows.

To start the following procedures, start the Windows Setup program from the Main program group.
Then choose the Options menu by pressing Alt+O
or by clicking Options.

To add or remove a group of files

1. Select Add/Remove Windows Components by
   pressing A and then Enter, or by clicking Add/
   Remove Windows Components. The Windows
   Setup dialog box appears.

2. Mark or unmark the following groups of files
   by clicking the corresponding check box or by
   pressing Alt+*letter*, where *letter* is F, A, G, S,
   or W:

   Readme Files
   Accessories
   Games
   Screen Savers
   Wallpapers, Misc.

   When a group's check box is marked, the files
   exist on the disk, and they take up the amount
   of space shown in the Bytes Used column. If a
   check box is unmarked, the files do not exist
   on the disk.

3. Press Enter or click OK to make the file changes. Click Cancel or press Esc to abandon changes.

To add individual files

1. Select Add/Remove Windows Components by pressing A and then Enter, or by clicking Add/ Remove Windows Components. The Windows Setup dialog box appears.

2. Press Tab and the arrow keys until the correct Files button is selected, or click the Files button. Then press Enter. Each Files button corresponds to an adjacent group of files. Those groups are as follows:

> Readme Files
> Accessories
> Games
> Screen Savers
> Wallpapers, Misc.

Another dialog box appears. The name of the dialog box reflects the group of files you chose.

3. Press Alt+N or click the files to add into the Do not install these files list box. Select the files to add to the hard disk.

4. Press Alt+A or click Add to move the selected files to the Install these files on the hard disk list box. The file name will move from the Do not install these files list box to the Install these files on the hard disk list box. You also can click Add All or press N to add all the files from the Do not install these files list box to the Install these files on the hard disk list box.

5. Press Enter or click OK to accept the changes.

6. Press Enter or click OK to accept the changes in the Windows Setup dialog box.

7. When instructed, place the correct Windows setup disk in the drive and press Enter or click OK. The files will be copied to the hard disk.

To remove individual files

1. Select Add/Remove Windows Components by pressing A and then Enter, or by clicking Add/ Remove Windows Components. The Windows Setup dialog box appears.

2. Press Tab and the arrow keys until the correct Files button is selected, or click the Files button. Then press Enter. Each Files button corresponds to an adjacent group of files. Those groups are as follows:

> Readme Files
> Accessories
> Games
> Screen Savers
> Wallpapers, Misc.

Another dialog box appears. The name of the dialog box reflects the group of files you chose.

3. Click the files to remove in the Install these files on the hard disk list box or press I. Select the files you want to remove from the hard disk.

4. Press Alt+R or click Remove to move the selected file to the Do not install these files list box. The file name will move from the Install these files on the hard disk list box to the Do not install these files list box.

5. Press Enter or click OK to accept the changes.

6. Press Enter or click OK to accept the changes in the Windows Setup dialog box.

7. When the Confirm Option Delete dialog box appears, click Yes or press Y to delete the selected files.

Notes

Several files that are not essential to the operation of Windows are stored in the Windows directory. All of these files take up nearly 2M disk space. (Accessories such as Write, Paint, and the Calculator take up approximately 1M.)

If you are running low on disk space, you can delete these nonessential files. If you did not install these files to begin with, or decide to put them on your computer once again, you can easily install them with the Windows Setup program.

You can add and remove the files as groups or as individual files. For quick results, add or remove the files in groups. However, if you want to use a few files from each group, add or remove the files individually.

Adding Program Groups

Program Manager

Purpose

Enables you to keep similar programs together. Use this option to create a new program group.

To add a program group

1. Make the Program Manager active.

2. Select the File menu by pressing Alt+F or by clicking File.

3. From the File menu, select New. The New Program Object dialog box appears.

4. Select Program Group.

5. Press Enter or click OK. The Program Group Properties dialog box appears.

6. Select the Description field and type the name of the new group.

   For example, type WORDPROCESSING.

7. If necessary, select the Group File field and type the name of the file you want to contain the new program group information. For example, type C:\WINDOWS\WORDPROC.GRP.

8. Press Enter or click OK to save the new program group.

Note

When you installed Windows, the following program groups may have been created: Main, Accessories, Applications, and Games. These groups logically separate different kinds of applications. You may decide, however, to create a program group that contains your word processing and accompanying applications. When you add a new program group, you must name the on-screen icon. Make sure that you do not duplicate a program group name or file name.

Adding Program Items

Program Manager

Purpose

Adds an icon to a program group so that you can start a program or batch file from this icon.

To add a program item

1. Open the Program Manager.

2. Press Alt+W or click the Window menu, and then open the program group to which you want to add the program item.

3. Choose the File menu by pressing Alt+F or by clicking File.

4. Choose the New option by pressing N or by clicking New. The New Program Object dialog box appears.

5. Select Program Item by pressing I or by clicking Program Item.

6. Press Enter or click OK. The Program Item Properties dialog box appears.

   To cancel the operation, press Esc or click Cancel.

7. Press Alt+D or click in the Description field. Type the name you want to appear under the icon.

   Suppose, for example, that you want to add Lotus 1-2-3. You might type LOTUS 1-2-3 for the description.

8. Press Alt+C or click Command Line. In the Command Line text box, type the name of the file that starts the program. You may have to include the path pointing to the file.

   Suppose, for example, that you created a PIF for Lotus 1-2-3 and stored the PIF in C:\123. Type C:\123\123.PIF.

   If you do not know the name of the file, press Alt+B or click the Browse button. The Browse dialog box lists files you can choose.

9. Press Alt+W or click Working Directory. Type the name of the directory where the data files are located. If you leave this area blank, the default location is the location of the starting program.

10. Press Alt+S or click Shortcut Key. Type a key combination you can use to quickly select the program when it is open on the desktop.

11. Select Run Minimized to start the program as an icon rather than as a Window.

12. To change the icon, press Alt+I or click the Change Icon button. The Select Icon dialog box appears.

13. Press Alt+F or click in the File Name field. Type PROGMAN.EXE or MORICONS.DLL.

14. Choose the icon to use from the Current Icon box. Either click in the scroll bar or use the arrow keys to select another icon.

15. To finish adding the program item, press Enter or click OK.

    To cancel the operation, press Esc or click Cancel.

Note

Each program in a program group is displayed as an icon and called a *program item*. When you installed Windows, several program items were created for you. For example, the Accessories program group contains the following program items: Write, Paintbrush, Terminal, Notepad, Recorder, Cardfile, Calendar, Calculator, Clock, Object Packager, Character Map, Media Player, and Sound Recorder.

Application Installation

Setup

Purpose

Searches your hard disk for programs you already installed.

To start the following procedures, open the Main program group from the Program Manager. Then select Windows Setup by choosing the icon with ← or → and pressing Enter, or double-click the Windows Setup icon.

To search for applications to install

1. From Windows Setup, select Options.

2. Select Set Up Applications.

3. Select Search for applications and press Enter or click OK. The Setup Applications dialog box appears.

4. Select to search only the Path or select the drive to search.

5. Select Search Now by pressing Enter or clicking Search Now.

6. From the list of programs under Applications found on hard disk(s), select the applications for use with Windows.

7. Select Add to specify the applications chosen or select Add All.

8. Press Tab until OK is highlighted, then press Enter. Or click OK

To install specific applications

1. From Windows Setup, select Options.

2. Select Set Up Applications.

3. Select Ask you to specify an application and press Enter or click OK. The Setup Applications dialog box appears.

4. In the Applications Path and Filename text box, type the path and name of the application. For example, to search for Write in the C:\Windows directory, type C:\WINDOWS\WRITE.EXE.

   If you are not sure of the path and the file name, choose Browse by pressing Alt+B or by clicking Browse.

5. Select the Add to program group list box by
    pressing Alt+A or by clicking the drop-down
    list arrow.

6. Select the program group you want to add the
    application to, using the arrow keys or clicking
    the group.

7. Press Enter or click OK to add the program to
    the group you selected.

To exit from Windows Setup

1. Select Options.

2. Select Exit.

Notes

Using this Setup option enables you to install
programs to run in Windows. When Setup installs
applications, it creates a list of the programs that it
finds. You then select the application you want to
set up as a program item, creating an icon for the
program. If the program is a non-Windows program,
then a PIF is created for the program.

When Windows does not find a program, you must
manually add the program. See *386 Enhanced
mode-PIF Editor*, *Standard Mode-PIF Editor*, and
Adding Program Items-Program Manager.

Arranging Icons

Program Manager

Purpose

Arranges icons in a program group window so that
you can see each icon. Sets up each program group

window so that the icons automatically are
arranged.

To move an icon using a mouse

1. Point to the icon and press and hold the left
   mouse button.

2. Drag the mouse until the icon is in the desired
   location.

3. Release the mouse button.

To arrange all icons in a window

1. Select the window that contains the icons you
   want to arrange.

2. Select the Window menu by pressing Alt+W or
   by pointing and clicking with the mouse.

3. Select Arrange Icons.

To set up the program manager so that all icons are arranged automatically

1. From the Program Manager, select Options.

2. Select Auto Arrange. A check mark appears
   next to the option after it is selected.

Note

When a program group window is open, icons can
become disarrayed so that you cannot see which
applications reside in the program group. The
arrangement of the icons depends on the shape of
the window. Suppose, for example, that the window
is tall and thin. The icons are arranged in columns.
If the window is short and wide, however, the icons
are arranged in rows. You may notice that when you
arrange icons, some of the icon names overlap. You

can change the spacing of icons, or you can edit the icon names so that they do not overlap. See *Desktop Customization*.

Arranging the Desktop

Task Manager

Purpose

Arranges icons and open windows on the desktop.

To arrange icons

1. Press Ctrl+Esc or double-click on the desktop. The Task List appears.

2. Press Alt+A or click Arrange Icons.

To tile windows

1. Press Ctrl+Esc or double-click on the desktop. The Task List appears.

2. Press Alt+T or click Tile.

To cascade windows

1. Press Ctrl+Esc or double-click on the desktop. The Task List appears.

2. Press Alt+C or click Cascade.

Notes

With Windows, you can have many windows open at a time on the desktop. However, if you open several windows, the desktop tends to get cluttered, and some windows may hide other windows and icons.

If your Windows desktop becomes cluttered, you can arrange the desktop. You may choose to arrange icons, or to tile or cascade windows. Tiling windows makes each open window the same size, and places windows next to each other. Cascading windows also makes each window the same size; however, the windows are overlapped in diagonal order. When windows are cascaded, you can easily select each window's title bar with the mouse.

Arranging Windows

Program Manager

Purpose

Arranges windows so that you can view more than one window at a time.

To move a window using a mouse

1. Activate the window by pointing to it and clicking.

2. Point to the title bar and press and hold the left mouse button.

3. As you drag the mouse, the window moves.

4. When the window is in a desired position, release the mouse button.

To move a window using the keyboard

1. Activate a window by pressing Alt+Esc.

2. Select the Control menu by pressing Alt+–.

3. Select Move.

4. Using the arrow keys, move the window to the desired position.

5. Press Enter when you have the window in the
   desired position.

Note

You can arrange windows so that the window
you want to reference is not overlapped by other
windows. You can keep windows small and place
them side-by-side. Maximize the window located in
the foreground, and minimize the window that is
not in use. The term for this method is *tiling*. The
second method keeps all the windows the same size,
but stair-steps each window. The term for this
method is *cascading*.

Associate Files

File Manager

Purpose

Starts an application when you choose an
application's data file.

To associate a file to a program

1. Start the File Manager from the Main program
   group.

2. Using the arrow keys, select the directory that
   contains the file to associate by highlighting
   the name and pressing Enter. Or point to the
   directory and click the mouse. A list of files
   appears in the contents list.

3. Select a file by pressing the arrow keys to highlight the name or by clicking the file name.

4. Choose the File menu.

5. Choose Associate. The Associate dialog box
   appears.

> Note: Files are associated based on their file extensions. For example, you can associate files with the ASC extension to the Notepad accessory. In the Associate dialog box, the extension you have selected to associate is shown in the Files with Extension text box. Select the Files with Extension text box to type a new extension to associate.

6. Select the Associate With list box.

7. Select the program to associate the file with by using the arrow keys or by clicking the program description.

> Note: If the program is not listed in the Associate With list box, choose the Browse button and search for the correct program.

8. Press Enter or click OK. Press Esc or click Cancel to abandon the selection.

To start a program using an associated file

1. Start the File Manager from the Main program group.

2. Press the arrow keys to select the directory with the associated file and press Enter. Or point to the directory that contains the associated file and click the mouse. A list of files appears in the contents list.

3. Press the arrow keys to select the correct file and press Enter. Or point to the file and double-click the mouse.

   If the file has been correctly associated, the associated program starts, and the file is retrieved into the program.

Notes

You can specify that when certain files are selected,
their respectful applications start. For example, you
can specify that files with the extension NTE start
Windows' Notepad accessory. When you select a file
with an NTE extension, Notepad starts and the file is
ready for editing.

Associated files are easy to spot in the File Manager.
An associated file is displayed with a document file
icon—a page with a folded corner.

Changing Colors

Control Panel

Purpose

Enables you to use different colors so that you can
customize the screen colors.

To begin selecting colors

1. Start the Control Panel from the Main program
   group.

2. Choose the Settings menu.

3. Choose Color.

To select a new color scheme

1. From the Color dialog box, select Color
   Schemes by pressing S or clicking the drop-
   down list arrow. A list box appears.

2. Press ↑ or ↓ and press Enter, or point to the
   correct scheme and click the mouse.

To change the color of an element of the screen

1. From the Color dialog box, choose Color Palette by pressing Alt+P or clicking the Color
   Palette button.

2. Choose Screen Element by pressing Alt+E or
   clicking the drop-down list arrow.

3. Press ↑ or ↓ to select the correct screen element and then press Enter. Or point to the
   correct element and click the mouse.

   > Note: If you are using a mouse, rather than
   > selecting the screen element from the list,
   > you may point to the screen element on
   > the representation of the screen in the
   > Color dialog box and click.

4. Choose Basic Colors by pressing Alt+B, or by
   pointing to one of the colors and clicking.

5. Press ↑ or ↓ to choose the correct color for
   the element, and then press the space bar. Or
   point to the correct color and click the mouse.

To define custom colors

1. Choose Custom Colors by pressing Alt+C or
   clicking a custom color box.

2. Choose Define Custom Colors. The Custom
   Color Selector dialog box appears.

3. Choose Hue, Sat, Lum, Red, Green, or Blue.
   These settings enable you to mix the three
   colors and set the brightness and richness of
   the overall color.

4. Type the value of the setting. If you are using a
   mouse, click the scroll boxes to change the
   values.

   Note that you can point to a position in the
   color box to select a custom color, rather

than typing values for Hue, Sat, Lum, Red, Green or Blue.

5. To save the custom color and continue creating new colors, choose Add Color by pressing Alt+A, or clicking the Add Color button.

   To save the custom color and stop creating custom colors, choose Close by pressing Alt+C or clicking the Close button.

To save a custom color scheme

1. Select the correct colors for each screen element as described in the preceding instructions.

2. Choose Save Scheme by pressing Alt+A or clicking the Save Scheme button.

3. Type the name of the new color scheme in the Save Scheme dialog box.

4. Press Enter or click OK.

To quit making color changes

1. Press Tab until the OK button is selected, then press Enter. Or click OK.

2. Choose Cancel to abandon the changes you made to the colors. Press Tab until the Cancel button is selected, then press Enter. Or click the Cancel button.

Notes

Choose colors to make each Window easy to identify. For example, you should see at a glance which window is active, what the title of the active window is, and what the contents of each visible window are.

You can pick from the standard colors in the Windows palette, or custom-create your own color variations. You can save a set of colors so that you can change from set to set of colors.

As you set colors, watch the sample screen in the Color dialog box to critique the mixture. Remember that some colors change appearance when other colors are added around them.

Changing DOS Fonts

Non-Window Programs

Purpose

Changes the font that characters display as you are working in a windowed DOS session.

To change fonts

1. Activate the non-Windows application by pressing Alt+Tab until the application appears in the foreground, or by clicking the application window with the mouse.

2. Choose the Control menu by pressing Alt+space bar or by clicking the Control menu box.

3. Choose Fonts by pressing F or by clicking Fonts on the Control menu. The Font Selection dialog box appears.

4. Press Alt+F or click a selection in the Font list box. You may use the scroll bars to select different font sizes in the Font list box.

The 8 x 12 selection means that each character is 8 screen pixels wide and 12 screen pixels high.

> Note: When you select a font, the actual size of the font is displayed in the Selected Font area of the Font Selection dialog box. The actual size of the DOS window can be viewed in the Window Preview area of the Font Selection dialog box. The Window Preview area shows how much of the screen the DOS window will take up.

5. Press Alt+S or click the Save Settings on Exit check box to make the font selection the default font selection for the current and future DOS windows.

6. Press Enter or click OK to accept the changes. Click Cancel or press Esc to abandon the changes.

Notes

You can change the size that characters display in a DOS window. You can change a character from a small 4-by-6 pixels to a large 16-by-12 pixels. You may find that the normal 8-by-8-pixel character is quite adequate. However, if you want to view more than one DOS window on the screen, you will need to make the characters smaller.

Some VGA displays enable you to view a Windows screen at a resolution of 800-by-600. The standard 8-by-8-pixel DOS character may be too small for you to read. In this case, you can change the font to an 8-by-12-pixel font. Experiment with the character sizes to find the right font size for your screen resolution.

Changing DOS Settings

Non-Window Programs

Purpose

Changes settings that control operations of a non-Windows program operating in the Windows environment.

To change DOS settings

1. Activate the non-Windows application by pressing Alt+Tab until the application appears in the foreground, or by clicking the application window with the mouse.

2. Choose the Control menu by pressing Alt+space bar or by clicking the Control menu box.

3. Choose Settings by pressing Alt+T or by clicking Settings from the Control menu. The DOS Window dialog box appears.

4. Press Alt+W or click the Window option button to display the non-Windows application in a window.

5. Press Alt+U or click the Full Screen option button to display the non-Windows application full-screen.

6. Press Alt+X or click the Exclusive check box to run the non-Windows application in exclusive mode.

7. Press Alt+B or click the Background check box to run the non-Windows application in the background while another application is operating in the foreground.

8. Select the Foreground text box by pressing Alt+F or by double-clicking in the text box.

9. Type the new Foreground value, a number from 1 to 10,000.

10. Select the Background text box by pressing Alt+A or by double-clicking in the text box.

11. Type the new Background value, a number from 1 to 10,000.

12. Press Enter or click OK to accept the changes. Click Cancel or press Esc to abandon the changes.

Notes

By changing the settings, you alter the way a non-windows application operates in the Windows environment. You can increase or decrease the amount of time that a non-Windows application has for operation when the application is in the fore-ground or background. You can also change the settings so that the program operates when it is in the foreground only. Or, you can allocate additional resources to the application when it is running full-screen. Changes that you make to the settings alter the way that Windows programs operate, too.

When you change the settings of a non-Windows application, the settings are in effect only for the specific non-Windows application—not for other non-Windows applications. Also, when you start the non-Windows application in a different session, the settings will return to the default settings of the PIF.

Use the Terminate button in the DOS Window dialog box with caution. This button stops all processing of the non-Windows application and removes the application from memory. If the data processed by the non-Windows application has not been saved, the data may be lost. If the application has not been closed properly, files may be corrupted. Normally, if you use this button, you should close Windows and reboot your computer before continuing.

Clipboard

Clipboard

Purpose

Stores text or graphics while you transfer them between two applications.

To store information in the Clipboard

1. From a Windows application, select the text or graphics to place in the Clipboard.

2. Choose the Edit menu by pressing Alt+E or by clicking Edit.

3. Choose Cut to remove the text or graphics from the application and place them in the Clipboard. Choose Copy to place a copy of the text or graphics in the Clipboard without removing the text or graphics from the application.

To start the Clipboard

1. From the Program Manager, open the Main program group.

2. From the Main program group, select Clipboard with the arrow keys and press Enter, or point to the Clipboard icon and double-click the mouse.

To save the Clipboard for later use

1. Start the Clipboard.

2. Choose the File menu by pressing Alt+F or by clicking File.

3. Choose Save As by pressing A or by clicking Save As. The File Save As dialog box appears.

4. Type the new name for the file. The default extension for the file is CLP.

5. To save the file in a different directory, choose Directories by pressing Alt+D, then select the directory in which you want to save the file.

   If you are using a mouse, point to the correct directory and click the mouse.

6. Press Tab until the OK button is selected and press Enter to save the file. If you are using a mouse, click OK.

   To cancel the save process, press Esc or click Cancel.

To open a Clipboard file

1. Start the Clipboard.

2. Choose the File menu by pressing Alt+F or by clicking File.

3. Choose Open by pressing O or by clicking Open. The File Open dialog box appears.

4. Type the new name for the file, or choose File Name and select the name of the file you want to open.

5. If you want to open a file from a different directory, choose Directories by pressing Alt+D, then select the directory to which you want to save the file. If you are using a mouse, point to the directory and click the mouse.

6. Press Tab until the OK button is selected and press Enter to open the file. If you are using a mouse, click OK.

   To cancel the file open process, press Esc or click Cancel.

To remove the contents of the Clipboard

1. Start the Clipboard.

2. Choose the Edit menu by pressing Alt+E or by clicking Edit.

3. Choose Delete by pressing D or by clicking Delete. The Clear Clipboard dialog box appears.

4. Press Enter or click Yes to clear the contents of the Clipboard.

   To cancel the clearing operation, press Tab until the No button is selected, and then press Enter. Or click No.

To change how text is viewed in the Clipboard

1. Start the Clipboard.

2. Choose the Display menu by pressing Alt+D or by clicking Display.

3. Choose Auto by pressing A or by clicking Auto.

   The text in the Clipboard takes on the same format that it had in the original application. You can choose one of the other options in the Display menu to vary the format of the text.

Note

If you are using Windows in 386 Enhanced mode, you can copy information not only from a non-Windows application to the Clipboard but from a Windows application to the Clipboard as well. Using the Print Screen key, you can copy the contents of the screen to the Clipboard. Simply press the Print Screen key; the screen is copied to the Clipboard. You can paste the screen into the Paint accessory for printing purposes.

Configure Serial Ports

Control Panel

Purpose

Configures any serial port so that a Windows application can communicate with a device, such as a printer or modem, attached to the port.

To start the following procedures, start the Control Panel from the Main program group. Then choose Ports from the Control Panel by selecting Ports with the arrow keys and pressing **Enter**, or by double-clicking the Ports icon.

To change the settings of a serial port

1. From the Ports dialog box, select the serial port you want to configure, using the arrow keys or by pressing **Alt+** *the port number*. Or point to the serial port and click the mouse.

2. Press **Alt+S** or click the Settings button. The Settings dialog box appears.

3. Press **Alt+B** or click the **Baud Rate** field.

4. Press **Alt+↓** or click the drop-down arrow button.

5. Press the arrow keys to select the correct Baud Rate setting, then press **Alt+↑** to choose the Baud Rate setting. Or click the correct Baud Rate setting.

6. Press **Alt+D**, then press ↑ and ↓ to choose the correct Data Bits setting. Or point to one of the Data Bits settings and click the mouse.

7. Press **Alt+P**, then press ↑ and ↓ to choose the correct Parity setting. Or point to one of the Parity settings and click the mouse.

8. Press Alt+S, then press ↑ and ↓ to choose Stop Bit settings. Or point to one of the Stop Bits settings and click the mouse.

9. Press Alt+F, then press ↑ and ↓ to choose the Flow Control settings. Or point to one of the Flow Control settings and click the mouse.

10. Press Enter or click OK to save the changes.

    To terminate the changes, press Esc or click Cancel.

11. From the Ports dialog box, press Enter or click Close.

To change the advanced settings of a serial port

1. From the Ports dialog box, select the serial port you want to configure, using the arrow keys or by pressing Alt+ *the port number*. Or point to the serial port and click the mouse.

2. Press Alt+S or click the Settings button.

3. Press Alt+A or click the Advanced button. The Advanced Settings dialog box appears.

4. Press Alt+B or click the Base I/O Port Address field.

5. Press Alt+↓ or click the drop-down list arrow.

6. Press the arrow keys to select the port address, then press Alt+↑ to choose the port address. Or click the correct port address.

7. Press Alt+I or click the Interrupt Request Line (IRQ) field.

8. Press Alt+↓ or click the drop-down list arrow.

9. Press the arrow keys to select the correct Interrupt request line, then press Alt+↑ to choose the Interrupt request line. Or click the correct Interrupt request.

10. Press Enter or click OK to save the changes.

    To terminate the changes, press Esc or click Cancel.

11. From the Settings dialog box, press Enter or click OK to save the changes.

    To terminate the changes, press Esc or click Cancel.

12. From the Ports dialog box, press Enter or click Close.

Notes

Before configuring a serial port, make sure that you know what the settings of the serial device must be. Consult the serial device's users manual for the proper settings.

Generally, you will not have to change the advanced setting for each communications port. Be careful. Selecting incorrect values can not only affect the serial port you are configuring, but can also affect other serial devices.

Configure Sound

Control Panel

Purpose

Changes the sound of an alarm for different Windows events. Toggles off sound completely, if desired.

To start the following procedures, start the Control Panel from the Main program group. Then choose the Settings menu by clicking Settings or by pressing Alt+S. Choose Sound from the Settings menu by clicking Sound or by pressing S. Or double-click the Sound icon.

To change a sound for an event

1. From the Sound dialog box, select the Events list by pressing Alt+E. Use the arrow keys to select the event. You also can click an event in the Events list box.

2. Select the Files list box by pressing Alt+F or by clicking a file in the Files list box. You can select files in the Files list box with the arrow keys.

3. Press Enter or click OK.

To test sounds

1. From the Sound dialog box, select a file in the Files list box. Do so by pressing Alt+F, then use the arrow keys. Or you can click a sound in the Files list box.

2. Press Alt+T to choose the Test button, then press Enter. Or click the Test button. Listen for the sound.

3. Press Esc or click Cancel when you have finished.

To disable and enable sounds

1. From the Sound dialog box, select Enable System Sounds. Either press Alt+N or click the Enable System Sounds check box. When the box is checked, the sounds are enabled.

2. Press Enter or click OK.

Notes

You can use the Sound option to attach different sounds to events such as displaying an error message or exiting Windows. You also can disable sounds altogether.

Sound files are listed with a WAV extension. Windows 3.1. comes with several sound files. You also can use sounds developed by others. Before you can use this option, however, you must have installed a Windows compatible sound board in your computer.

Copy a Disk

File Manager

Purpose

Duplicates an entire disk.

To start the following procedures, start the File Manager from the Main program group. Then choose the Disk menu by pressing Alt+D or by clicking Disk.

To copy a disk with a single disk drive

1. Choose Copy Disk by pressing C or by clicking Copy Disk. The Confirm Copy Disk dialog box appears.

2. To continue with Copy Disk, press Y or click the Yes button. To terminate Copy Disk, press N or click the No button.

3. If you chose the Yes button, the Copy Disk dialog box appears. You are instructed to insert the source disk. Place the disk to copy in the disk drive and press Enter or click OK.

4. When copying begins, the Copying Disk dialog box appears on-screen and displays the progress of the copy process. Press Esc or click Cancel to terminate the copy process.

5. The Copy Disk dialog box appears again. This time, you are instructed to insert the destination disk. Place the disk you want to copy to in the disk drive and press Enter or click OK.

6. The Copying Disk dialog box appears on-screen again and displays the progress of the copy process. Press Esc or click Cancel to terminate the copy process. When copying is completed, remove the destination disk from the disk drive.

To copy a disk

1. Choose Copy Disk by pressing C or by clicking Copy Disk. The Confirm Copy Disk dialog box appears.

2. Choose Source In by pressing Alt+S or by clicking in the Source In field.

3. Select the source drive letter.

4. Choose Destination In by pressing Alt+D or by clicking in the Destination In field.

5. Select the destination drive letter.

6. Press Tab to select OK, then press Enter or click OK.

7. When the Confirm Copy Disk dialog box appears, press Y then Enter or click Yes to continue the copy process. Press N then Enter or click No to terminate the copy process.

8. Windows instructs you to insert the source disk. Place the diskette into the source drive, then choose OK to continue the copy.

9. If you are prompted to change diskettes, do so. Press Enter or click OK to continue the copy process.

10. When the copy is complete, remove the last disk, and label the destination disk.

You can select Cancel to terminate the copy process.

Note

Always make backup copies of your program disks and work disks. File Manager's Copy Disk function easily enables you to create disk duplicates. When duplicating a disk, you must use disks of like capacity. If the disk you want to duplicate is a 5 1/4-inch high density disk, then the disk you copy to must be a 5 1/4-inch high density disk.

Copy Files

File Manager

Purpose

Duplicates individual files from the Main program group.

To copy file(s) from one drive to another drive using the keyboard

1. Start the File Manager from the Main program group.

2. Place the source disk and destination disk in the correct drives. For example, place the source disk in drive A and the destination disk in drive B.

If you are copying to or from a hard disk to a floppy disk, place the floppy disk in the drive.

3. Activate the source disk by pressing **Ctrl** and the letter associated with the drive.

   For example, press **Ctrl+A** to activate drive A.

4. Begin selecting the file or files you want to copy (see *Selecting Files*).

5. Choose the **File** menu by pressing **Alt+F**.

6. Choose **Copy** by pressing **C**.

7. When the Copy dialog box appears, type the name of the drive to which you want to copy.

   Suppose, for example, that you are copying to a disk in drive A. Type **B:**.

   Or

   Press **Alt+C** to choose the Copy to Clipboard option button. You copy a file to the Clipboard in order to link or embed the file into a document.

8. Press **Enter**.

   To terminate the copy process, press **Tab** until the Cancel button is selected, then press **Enter**.

To copy file(s) from one drive to another drive using the mouse

1. Start the File Manager.

2. Place the source disk and destination disk in the correct drives.

   For example, place the source disk in drive A and the destination disk in drive B.

3. Activate the source disk by clicking the drive icon.

4. Begin selecting the file or files to copy (see *Selecting Files*).

5. Point to the file icon of one of the selected files, and press and hold the left mouse button.

6. Drag the file icon to the destination drive or directory icon. Release the mouse button after you have the file icon positioned over the correct destination drive or directory icon. The Copying dialog box appears.

   You can click Cancel to terminate the copy process.

Notes

You can use the File Manager to copy files from one directory to another, from one disk to another, or between a hard disk and a floppy disk. If you are copying a file that already exists on the destination disk (the disk to which you are copying), make sure that the file can be overwritten. You can compare the file's dates and times.

Sometimes you will select more files to copy than a disk can hold. If the destination disk becomes full as you are copying files, you will be prompted to insert a new disk. Place a new disk in the drive and press R or click the Retry button. The files remaining will be copied to the new disk.

Create Directories

File Manager

Purpose

Enables you to create new subdirectories on your hard disk or diskette. This option is the equivalent of the DOS MD command.

To create a directory

1. Start the File Manager.

2. Select the drive you want to contain the directory by pressing **Ctrl** and the drive letter. For example, to select drive C, press **Ctrl+C**.

   Or

   Point to the drive icon with the mouse and click the left mouse button.

3. Select the directory in which you want to create a new subdirectory by pressing ↑ and ↓ in the Directory Tree window.

   Or

   Point to the directory in the Directory Tree window and click the mouse. You may have to expand a directory. (See *Expanding Directory Levels*.)

4. Choose the **F**ile menu.

5. Choose Create Directory. The Create Directory dialog box appears.

   Make sure that the Create Directory box shows the correct path. Suppose, for example, that you want to create a subdirectory of C:\DATA. Make sure that C:\DATA appears in the dialog box.

6. Type the new subdirectory name. For example, type **123DATA**.

7. Press **Enter** or click **OK**.

   Choose **Cancel** to stop creating a directory.

Notes

When you create a directory, if you only type the directory name (for example NEWDIR), the directory is created as a subdirectory of the current directory.

If the current directory is C:\WORD, then the new directory will be C:\WORD\NEWDIR.

If you want to create a directory in a location other than the current directory, you can choose another directory as the current directory, or you can enter the entire path for the new directory. For example, if the current directory is C:\WORD and you want NEWDIR to be a subdirectory of the C:\DATABASE directory, then type the full path C:\DATABASE\NEWDIR.

Delete a Print Job

Print Manager

Purpose

Abandons a print job that is printing on the printer or is in line to be printed.

To delete a print job

1. If the application is sending data to the Print Manager, select Cancel in the printing dialog box.

2. Activate the Print Manager by pressing Alt+Tab until the Print Manager is selected. Then release both keys. When you release the Alt key, the Print Manager will display and, if minimized, will open as a window.

   If you are using a mouse, point to the Print Manager and double-click the mouse.

3. Press ↑ and ↓ to select the print job you want to delete. Or click the job with the mouse.

4. Choose the Delete button by pressing Alt+D or by clicking Delete.

Note

As you are printing in Windows, you may notice that your print job is not printing correctly. Rather than continuing or just pausing the print job, you may need to terminate the print job, deleting it from the Print Manager. Any data that has already been sent to the printer will continue to print even though the print job has been terminated.

Delete Files

File Manager

Purpose

Enables you to delete files from a disk.

To enable or disable confirmation

1. Start the File Manager from the Main program group.

2. From the File Manager, choose the Options menu.

3. Choose Confirmation. The Confirmation dialog box appears.

   Choosing File Delete toggles whether or not a dialog box appears when you delete a file.

   Choosing Directory Delete toggles whether or not a dialog box appears when you delete a subdirectory.

4. After you select the desired settings, press Enter or click OK.

To delete a file

1. Start the File Manager from the Main program group.

2. Press Ctrl and the letter of the drive that contains the file you want to delete. Suppose, for example, that you want to delete a file from drive C. Press Ctrl+C. If you are using a mouse, point to the disk drive icon and click the mouse.

3. Press the arrow keys to select the sub-directory you want to delete and press Enter. Or point to the subdirectory and click the mouse.

4. Select the files to delete (see *Selecting Files*).

5. Choose the File menu by pressing Alt+F or by clicking File.

6. Choose Delete by pressing D or clicking Delete. The Delete dialog box appears.

7. If the file shown in the Delete field is correct, choose Delete by pressing Enter or by clicking OK.

   To terminate delete, choose Cancel by pressing Esc or by clicking Cancel.

   > Note: This step only occurs if you have selected Confirmation from the Options menu and enabled File Delete in the Confirmation dialog box.

8. The File Manager dialog box appears so that you can verify that you really want to delete the file. Select Yes to delete the file by pressing Y or by clicking Yes.

   If you select more than one file, select Yes to All by pressing A or by clicking Yes to All.

Select No or Cancel to terminate the operation by pressing N or Esc, or by clicking either the No or Cancel button.

To delete a subdirectory

1. Start the File Manager from the Main program group.

2. Press Ctrl and the letter of the drive that contains the subdirectory you want to delete. Suppose, for example, that you want to delete a file from drive C. Press Ctrl+C. If you are using a mouse, point to the disk drive icon and click the mouse.

3. Press the arrow keys to select the subdirectory you want to delete and press Enter, or point to the subdirectory and click the mouse.

4. Choose the File menu by pressing Alt+F or by clicking File.

5. Choose Delete by pressing D or by clicking Delete. The Delete dialog box appears.

6. If the subdirectory shown in the Delete field is correct, choose Delete by pressing Enter or by clicking OK.

   To terminate delete, choose Cancel by pressing Esc or by clicking Cancel.

7. The File Manager dialog box appears so that you can verify that you really want to delete the subdirectory. Select Yes to delete the subdirectory by pressing Y or by clicking Yes.

   Select No or Cancel to terminate the operation by pressing N or Esc, or by clicking either the No or Cancel button.

Note

When you no longer need a file or subdirectory or need to make room on a disk, you can delete unnecessary files and subdirectories. Windows enables you to select files for deletion even if their names have nothing in common. Windows also enables you to delete subdirectories even if they have other subdirectories or files contained within them.

Deleting Program Groups

Program Manager

Purpose

Deletes a program group and its associated icon from the Program Manager.

To delete a program group

1. Activate the Program Manager.

2. Choose the Window menu by pressing Alt+W or by clicking Window.

3. Choose the numbered option associated with the program group you want to delete by pressing the option number or by pointing to the option and clicking the mouse.

4. Minimize the program group window by choosing the program group's Control menu. Then choose Minimize or click the Minimize button.

5. Choose the File menu by pressing Alt+F or by clicking File.

6. Choose Delete by pressing D or by clicking
   Delete. The Delete dialog box appears.

   Note: You can press Del rather than
   performing steps 5 and 6.

7. Confirm the deletion by pressing Y or by
   clicking Yes.

   You can choose not to complete the deletion
   by pressing N or clicking No.

Note

You must use caution when deleting a program
group. If there are any program items contained in
the program group, they will be deleted as well.

Deleting Program Items

Program Manager

Purpose

Removes a program item from a program group
when you no longer use an application.

To delete a program item

1. Activate the Program Manager.

2. Choose the Window menu by pressing Alt+W
   or by clicking Window.

3. Choose the numbered option associated with
   the program group that contains the program
   item you want to delete by pressing the option
   number or by pointing to the option and clicking the mouse.

4. Select the program item to delete by pressing the arrow keys or by clicking the program item.

5. Choose the File menu by pressing Alt+F or by clicking File.

6. Choose Delete by pressing D or by clicking Delete. The Delete dialog box appears.

   Note: You can press Del rather than performing steps 5 and 6.

7. To confirm the deletion, choose Yes by pressing Y or by clicking Yes.

   You can choose not to complete the deletion by pressing N or clicking No.

Note

Use care when deleting a program item. Although you can add back a program item, you will save yourself time and frustration by making sure that the correct program item is selected for deletion.

Desktop Customization

Control Panel

Purpose

Enables you to use several options to customize the Desktop. You can change the pattern of the Desktop, or attach a bit-mapped file as "wallpaper"; customize the blink rate of the cursor; and change the spacing of icons in the Program Manager. You can change the size of each window's border and the grid for sizing windows. Also, you can enable and modify options for the screen saver.

Before you change any of the Desktop options, you first must start the Control Panel, choose the Settings menu, and then choose the Desktop option.

To change the Desktop pattern

1. Start the Control Panel from the Main program group.

2. From the Control Panel, open Desktop by choosing Settings Desktop. Or double-click the Desktop icon. The Desktop dialog box appears.

3. Choose Pattern Name by pressing Alt+N or by clicking the Name field.

4. To view the available patterns, choose the drop-down list box by pressing Alt+↓, or by clicking the drop-down list arrow.

5. To select the desired pattern, press ↑ and ↓, and then press Alt+↑. Or click the scroll bar until the desired pattern is in view, point to the pattern, and click the mouse.

To add a new Desktop pattern (mouse only)

1. From the Desktop dialog box, click Edit Pattern.

2. Click the drop-down list box to select the pattern that is similar to the pattern you want to add, and click the pattern name.

3. Type the new pattern name in the Name text box.

4. Point to the pattern box and click the mouse to change the pattern.

5. Click the Add button to save the changes to the new pattern name.

6. Click Close to save the new pattern. Click Cancel to terminate the new pattern.

To edit the Desktop pattern (mouse only)

1. From the Desktop dialog box, click Edit
   Pattern.

2. Click the drop-down list box to select the pattern to edit, and click the pattern name.

3. Point to the pattern box and click the mouse to
   change the pattern.

4. Click the Change button to save the changes to
   the assigned name.

5. Click Close to save the changes to the pattern.
   Click Cancel to terminate the pattern changes.

To remove a Desktop pattern

1. From the Desktop dialog box, choose Edit
   Pattern by pressing Alt+P or by clicking Edit
   Pattern.

2. Choose the drop-down list box by pressing
   Alt+↓ or by clicking the drop-down list box.
   Select the pattern you want to remove by using the arrow keys or by clicking the pattern
   name.

3. Choose the Remove button by pressing Alt+R
   or by clicking Remove.

4. When you are prompted to confirm the operation, press Y or click the Yes button to remove
   the pattern; or, if you do not want to remove
   the pattern, press N or click the No button.

5. Choose Close by pressing Enter or by clicking
   Close.

   Choose Cancel by pressing Esc or by clicking
   Cancel to terminate removing the pattern.

To change fast task-switching

From the Desktop dialog box, select Fast "Alt+Tab" Switching by pressing Alt+I or by clicking the Fast "Alt+Tab" Switching check box. When the check box is marked, you can quickly switch from one application to another by pressing Alt+Tab.

To change the screen saver

1. From the Desktop dialog box, select Name by pressing Alt+A or by clicking in the Name field.

2. Press Alt+↓ or click the drop-down list arrow to display the screen savers available.

3. Using the arrow keys, select the screen saver you want to use. Or click the screen saver you want to use.

4. Test the screen saver by pressing Alt+E or by clicking the Test button. Press Enter or click the mouse to stop the test.

5. Select the Delay field by pressing Alt+D or by clicking in the Delay field.

6. Use the arrow keys to select the number of minutes before the screen saver is activated.

7. You can alter settings to most screen savers. Choose the Setup button by pressing Alt+U or by clicking Setup. Make any necessary changes, and click OK or press Enter to return to the Desktop dialog box.

8. Press Enter or click OK to accept the changes.

To change the Desktop wallpaper

1. From the Desktop dialog box, select Wallpaper File by pressing Alt+F or by clicking in the File field.

2. Choose the File drop-down list box by pressing Alt+↓ or by clicking the drop-down list box.

3. To choose the wallpaper file, press the arrow keys and then press Alt+↑. Or point to the wallpaper file and click the mouse.

4. To place the wallpaper in the center of the screen, select Center by pressing Alt+C or by clicking Center.

5. To place the wallpaper side-by-side on the screen, select Tile by pressing Alt+T or by clicking Tile.

To change the cursor blink rate

1. From the Desktop dialog box, select Cursor Blink Rate by pressing Alt+R or by clicking the Cursor Blink Rate scroll bar.

2. Change the blink rate in one of these ways:

   ■ Press ← and →.

   ■ Point to the scroll box with the mouse, press and hold the left mouse button, drag the scroll box to the desired position, and release the mouse button.

   ■ Point to the scroll arrows with the mouse and click until the scroll box is in the desired position.

   As you adjust the position of the scroll box, the gray shadow blinks at the rate that the cursor will blink.

To change the icon spacing

1. From the Desktop dialog box, select Spacing by pressing Alt+S or by clicking in the Spacing field.

2. Change the spacing to a pixel value between 32 and 512 by typing the new number or by pointing to the scroll arrows and clicking the mouse until the desired number appears in the field.

3. Press Alt+W or click the Wrap Title check box to enable a long icon title to wrap to additional lines.

To change the grid on which a window is sized

1. From the Desktop dialog box, select Granularity by pressing Alt+G or by clicking in the Granularity field.

2. Change the granularity to a value between 0 and 49 by typing the new number, or by pointing to the scroll arrows and clicking the mouse until the desired number appears in the field.

To change the border width

1. From the Desktop dialog box, select Border Width by pressing Alt+B, or by clicking in the Border Width field.

2. Change the border width to a value between 1 and 50 by typing the new number, or by pointing to the scroll arrows and clicking the mouse until the desired number appears in the field.

Notes

You can experiment with the Desktop options. Although these options change many features of the Windows' Desktop, nothing that you change can cause adverse consequences. You can return each option, when modified, to its original setting.

Directory Tree Usage

File Manager

Purpose

Lists all the subdirectories on the current disk drive.
From the Directory Tree window, you can expand
and collapse each subdirectory branch. In addition,
you can open a subdirectory window (folder) so
that you can see all the subdirectories and files that
the subdirectory contains.

To select a disk drive

1. Start the File Manager from the Main program
   group.

2. To select a different disk drive, press Ctrl and
   the letter that corresponds to the disk drive.
   Suppose, for example, that you want to select
   disk drive A. Press Ctrl+A. If you are using a
   mouse, point to the disk drive icon and click
   the mouse.

To select a subdirectory using the keyboard

1. Start the File Manager from the Main program
   group.

2. With the Directory Tree window active, press
   ↑ and ↓ to move the highlight to the correct
   subdirectory. The window will scroll as
   necessary.

To select a subdirectory using the mouse

1. Start the File Manager from the Main program group.

2. Activate the Directory Tree window. Press and hold the left mouse button and drag the scroll box until the desired subdirectory is in view. Release the mouse button.

3. Point to the desired subdirectory and click the mouse.

To expand one level of a subdirectory branch using the keyboard

1. Start the File Manager from the Main program group.

2. With the Directory Tree window active, select the subdirectory that contains the branch you want to expand one level.

3. Choose the Tree menu by pressing Alt+T.

4. Choose Expand One Level by pressing E.

 **Note:** You can press + rather than perform steps 3 and 4.

To expand one level of a subdirectory branch using the mouse

1. Start the File Manager from the Main program group.

2. With the Directory Tree window active, point to the scroll box, press and hold the left mouse button, and drag the scroll box until the desired subdirectory is in view. Release the mouse button.

3. Point to the desired subdirectory that contains an icon with a plus, and double-click the mouse.

To expand an entire subdirectory branch

1. Start the File Manager from the Main program group.

2. With the Directory Tree window active, select the subdirectory that contains the branch you want to expand.

3. Choose the Tree menu by pressing Alt+T or by clicking Tree.

4. Choose Expand Branch by pressing B or by clicking Expand Branch.

   Note: You can press * rather than perform steps 3 and 4.

To expand all subdirectory branches

1. Start the File Manager from the Main program group.

2. Make the Directory Tree window active.

3. Choose the Tree menu by pressing Alt+T or by clicking Tree.

4. Choose Expand All by pressing A or by clicking Expand All.

   Note: You can press Ctrl+* rather than follow steps 3 and 4.

To collapse an entire subdirectory branch

1. Start the File Manager from the Main program group.

2. With the Directory Tree window active, select the subdirectory that contains the branch you want to collapse.

3. Choose the Tree menu by pressing Alt+T or by clicking Tree.

4. Choose Collapse Branch by pressing C or by clicking Collapse Branch.

   Note: You can press – rather than follow steps 3 and 4.

To display expandable and collapsible branches graphically

1. Choose the Tree menu by pressing Alt+T or by clicking Tree.

2. Choose Indicate Expandable Branches by pressing I or by clicking Indicate Expandable Branches. When a check mark is next to Indicate Expandable Branches, the option has been selected. Expandable branches display with a plus (+) in the directory icon. Collapsible branches display with a minus (-) in the directory icon.

Notes

The Directory Tree window is the main window you use; it is also the first window you see when you start the File Manager.

Subdirectories are among the hardest concepts for most new users to grasp. However, using the

Directory Tree window, you can see what a subdirectory does and where each subdirectory actually resides in relation to other subdirectories.

If you do not see a subdirectory you think should be displayed in the Directory Tree window, you can collapse a subdirectory branch to display only the upper-level subdirectory. You may have to use the scroll bars to view additional subdirectories and subdirectory branches.

Directory Window Usage

File Manager

Purpose

Adds a window to display other drives or directories. Also, changes the size of the directory tree and contents list in the directory window.

To add a directory window

1. Start the File Manager application.

2. Choose the Window menu by pressing Alt+W or by clicking Window.

3. Choose New Window from the Window menu by pressing N or by clicking New Window. A new directory window appears on the screen.

To close a directory window

1. From the File Manager, activate the directory window you want to close by pressing Ctrl+F6 until the window is active, or by clicking the window.

2. Press Alt+– or click Document control.

3. Choose Close from the Control menu by pressing C or by clicking Close.

> Note: You can press Ctrl+F4 rather than perform steps 2 and 3 above.

To change the split of a directory window

1. From the File Manager, activate the directory window you want to split by pressing Ctrl+F6 until the window to split is active, or by clicking the window.

2. Choose the View menu by pressing Alt+V or by clicking View.

3. Choose Split from the View menu by pressing L or by clicking Split. A dark vertical line appears in the directory window.

4. Change the split of the window by moving the mouse or by pressing ← or →.

5. To accept the split, click the mouse or press Enter.

Notes

Sometimes you may want to view the contents of two directories at once—especially if you plan to copy files from a directory on one drive to a directory on a second drive. To view an additional directory, you must create another directory window.

If a directory contains many files and you want to display more files on-screen than can be seen, you can increase the size of the files window. Conversely, if you want the directory window to be larger than the files window, you can increase the size of the directory window.

Expanding Directory Levels

File Manager

Purpose

Modifies the Directory Tree window so that
you can see all subdirectories or only levels of
subdirectories. Expands directory levels so that
you can see more than just first level directories.

To expand one level of a subdirectory branch using the keyboard

1. With the Directory Tree window active, select
   the subdirectory that contains the branch you
   want to expand one level.

2. Choose the Tree menu by pressing Alt+T.

3. Choose Expand One Level by pressing X.

   Note: You can press + rather than follow
   steps 2 and 3.

To expand one level of a subdirectory branch using the mouse

1. With the Directory Tree window active, point
   to the scroll box with the mouse, press and
   hold the left mouse button, and drag the scroll
   box until the desired subdirectory is in view.
   Release the mouse button.

2. Point to the desired subdirectory that contains
   an icon with a plus and double-click the
   mouse.

To expand an entire subdirectory branch

1. With the Directory Tree window active, select the subdirectory that contains the branch you want to expand.

2. Choose the Tree menu by pressing Alt+T or by clicking Tree.

3. Choose Expand Branch by pressing B.

> Note: You can press * rather than follow steps 2 and 3.

To expand all subdirectory branches

1. With the Directory Tree window active, select the subdirectory that contains the branch you want to expand.

2. Choose the Tree menu by pressing Alt+T or by clicking Tree.

3. Choose Expand All by pressing A.

> Note: You can press Ctrl+* rather than follow steps 2 and 3.

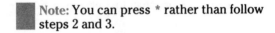

Font Selection

Control Panel

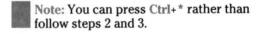

Purpose

Enables you to add and remove fonts from the operating environment.

To start the following procedures, start the Control Panel from the Main program group. Then start

Fonts by selecting the Fonts icon with the arrow keys and pressing Enter or by double-clicking the Fonts icon.

To add fonts to Windows

1. From the Fonts dialog box, choose Add by pressing Alt+A or by clicking Add.

2. When the Add Font Files dialog box appears, choose Drives by pressing Alt+V. Using the arrow keys or the mouse, select the drive containing the new fonts.

3. Press Alt+D to choose directories, press the arrow keys to select the correct drive and directory, and press Enter. Or point to the correct drive or directory and click the mouse.

4. Select List of Fonts by pressing Alt+F. Press the arrow keys to select the font files (pressing the space bar if the select bar is an outline rather than a highlight), and then press Enter.

   If you are using a mouse, point to the correct font file and double-click the mouse. If the font is already installed, then a message dialog box appears, and you see Font already installed.

   Press Enter or click OK to continue.

   Or

   To add all the fonts in the List of Fonts list box, choose Select All by pressing Alt+S or by clicking Select All.

5. Select the Copy Fonts to Windows Directory check box by pressing Alt+C or by clicking the Copy Fonts to Windows Directory check box. When the check box is selected, all fonts will be copied to the directory that contains Windows.

6. Choose OK by pressing Enter or by clicking OK.

To remove fonts from Windows

1. From the Fonts dialog box, press Alt+F, using the arrow keys to select the font you want to remove.

   If you are using a mouse, point to the font you want to remove and click the mouse.

2. Choose Remove by pressing Alt+R or by clicking Remove. The Remove Font dialog box appears.

3. Select the Delete Font File From Disk check box to remove the file from the disk after the font has been removed from Windows.

4. Choose Yes to remove the font by pressing Y or clicking Yes.

   To terminate this procedure, choose No by pressing N or by clicking No.

5. Choose OK by pressing Enter or clicking OK.

Notes

Windows is a what-you-see-is-what-you-get environment. That is, what you see on-screen basically is what you will see on the printed page. Programs written to take advantage of the Windows environment can access these fonts, whereas non-Windows programs are not designed to access them. You must be able to see different fonts on-screen, however. A font is a combination of the typeface and typesize of the characters you use in a document.

Windows can support different fonts, including TrueType fonts. You may find that you want to add fonts to the operating environment. Note that when you add a font to Windows, you use disk space (however, TrueType fonts take up much less space than bit-map fonts). If you are running short on disk space, you can temporarily remove fonts that you use on a non-continuous basis.

Format a Disk

Purpose

Prepares a new disk for use with the computer.

To format a disk

1. Start the File Manager.

2. Choose the Disk menu by pressing Alt+D or by clicking Disk.

3. Choose Format Diskette by pressing F or by clicking Format Diskette. The Format Diskette dialog box appears.

4. Choose the Disk In drop-down list box by pressing Alt+↓ or by clicking the Disk In drop-down list arrow. The list of disk drives appears.

5. To choose the drive you want to use, press the arrow keys and press Enter. Or click the drive.

6. Choose the Capacity drop-down list box by pressing Alt+↓ or by clicking the Capacity drop-down list arrow. The list of disk capacities appears.

7. To choose the capacity you want to use, press the arrow keys and press Enter. Or click the disk capacity.

8. To add a label to the disk, choose the Label text box. Type the label you want to use.

9. Select the Make System Disk check box by pressing M or by clicking the Make System Disk check box. This option is a toggle.

10. Select the Quick Format by pressing Q or by clicking the Quick Format check box. This option is a toggle. You only can quickly format a disk that previously has been formatted.

11. Press Enter or click OK.

    To terminate the disk format, press Esc or click Cancel.

12. If you chose to format a disk in drive A, this message appears in the Format Disk dialog box: Formatting will erase ALL data from your disk. Are you sure that you want to format the disk in Drive A:? To continue, press Enter or Y to choose Yes, or click the Yes button.

    To cancel the disk format, press N or click the No button.

13. You can press Esc to abort the format, or click Cancel.

14. This message appears in the Format Complete dialog box: Do you want to format another disk? Choose Yes by pressing Y, or choose No by pressing N. If you choose Yes, you return to step 4.

Notes

If your computer has more than one disk drive, be sure that you choose the correct drive in which to format a disk. If your computer has a high-density drive, verify whether you are formatting in a double-density or high-density drive.

When you select a disk in the File Manager by pressing Ctrl+*drive letter* or by clicking a drive icon, the File Manager checks the disk to see if it has ever been formatted. If the disk is determined to be unformatted, the File Manager prompts you to begin formatting the disk.

Hardware Settings

Purpose

Changes Windows so that it adapts to new hardware. When you add new hardware, you need to adjust Windows for the new display, keyboard, mouse, and network.

To start the following procedures, start Windows Setup from the Main program group. Then from the Windows Setup dialog box, choose the Options menu by pressing Alt+O or by clicking Options. Choose Change System Settings by pressing C or by clicking Change System Settings.

To change the type of display

1. From the Change System Settings dialog box, choose Display by pressing Alt+D or by clicking the Display field.

2. Choose the drop-down list box by pressing Alt+↓ or by clicking the drop-down list arrow.

3. Use the arrow keys to select the correct display type and press Enter. Or use the scroll bar to find the correct display, and then click the correct display type.

4. Follow the Windows prompts to insert the correct install disks.

5. Choose OK by pressing Enter or by clicking OK.

To change the type of keyboard

1. From the Change System Settings dialog box, choose Keyboard by pressing Alt+K or by clicking the Keyboard field.

2. Choose the drop-down list box by pressing Alt+↓ or by clicking the drop-down list arrow.

3. Use the arrow keys to select the correct keyboard type and press Enter. Or use the scroll bar to find the correct keyboard, and then click the keyboard type.

4. Follow the Windows prompts for inserting the correct install disks.

5. Choose OK by pressing Enter or by clicking OK.

To change the type of mouse

1. From the Change System Settings dialog box, choose Mouse by pressing Alt+M or by clicking the Mouse field.

2. Choose the drop-down list box by pressing Alt+↓ or by clicking the drop-down list arrow.

3. Use the arrow keys to select the correct mouse type and press Enter. Or use the scroll bar to find the correct mouse, and then click the mouse type.

4. Follow the Windows prompts to insert the correct install disks.

5. Choose OK by pressing Enter or by clicking OK.

To change the type of network

1. From the Change System Settings dialog box, choose Network by pressing Alt+N or by clicking the Network field.

2. Choose the drop-down list box by pressing Alt+↓ or by clicking the drop-down list arrow.

3. Use the arrow keys to select the correct network and press Enter. Or use the scroll bar to
   find the correct network, and then click the
   mouse.

4. Follow the Windows prompts to insert the
   correct install disks.

5. Choose OK by pressing Enter or by
   clicking OK.

Note

When you make changes to the Windows setup,
make sure that you select the correct devices.
Selecting an incorrect device might cause Windows
to function improperly or not function at all.

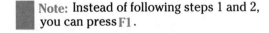

General

Purpose

Displays context-sensitive help.

To get the Help index

1. Select the H elp menu.
2. Select C ontents. The Help window appears.

> Note: Instead of following steps 1 and 2,
> you can press F1 .

To get help on the keyboard

1. Select the H elp menu.

2. Select Contents. The Help window appears.

3. Select one of the sections under the Keyboard heading.

To get help on commands

1. Select the Help menu.

2. Select Contents. The Help window appears.

3. Select one of the sections under the Commands heading.

To get help on procedures

1. Select the Help menu.

2. Select Contents. The Help window appears.

3. Select one of the sections under the How To heading.

To get help on Help

1. Select the Help menu.

2. Select How to use Help. The How To Use Help window appears on-screen.

To open a new Help file

1. Select the File menu.

2. Select Open. The File Open dialog box appears.

3. Select Drives by pressing Alt+V, and then change the drive if necessary. You normally use the default drive.

4. Select Directories by pressing Alt+D, and then change to the Windows subdirectory. Or point

to the correct directory and double-click the mouse to change directories.

5. Select File Name.

6. Select the correct Help file using ↑ and ↓, or by clicking the Help file with the mouse.

7. Press Enter or click OK to open the file.

   To terminate opening a file, press Esc or click Cancel.

To print a Help topic

1. Select the appropriate Help topic.

2. Select the File menu.

3. Select Print Topic.

4. When the Print dialog box appears, you can press Esc or click Cancel to terminate printing.

To add notes to a Help topic

1. Select the appropriate Help topic.

2. Select the Edit menu.

3. Select Annotate. The Help Annotate dialog box appears.

4. Select Annotation by pressing Alt+A or by clicking the Annotation field.

5. Type the notes you want to remember.

6. Press Alt+S or click Save to save the Annotation.

   To abandon the annotation, press Alt+F4 or click Cancel.

   If you do not abandon the annotation, a paper clip icon appears in the Help window.

While you type the annotation, you can select and copy the text to the Clipboard for use in another annotation or elsewhere in Windows. You also can paste text in the annotation box from the Clipboard.

To view an annotation using the keyboard

1. Select the Help topic that contains the annotation you want to view. A paper clip appears in the Help window.

2. Select the Edit menu.

3. Select Annotate.

   The note you previously typed appears in the Annotate dialog box.

To view an annotation using the mouse

1. Select the Help topic that contains the annotation you want to view. A paper clip appears in the Help window.

2. Click the paper clip icon.

To delete an annotation

1. Select the Help topic that contains the annotation you want to delete. A paper clip appears in the Help window.

2. Select the Edit menu.

3. Select Annotate. The Annotate dialog box appears.

4. Select Delete by pressing Alt+D or by clicking the Delete button.

To insert a bookmark in a Help topic

1. Select the Help topic.

2. Select the Bookmark menu.

3. Select Define. The Bookmark Define dialog box appears.

4. Select Bookmark Name by pressing Alt+B or by clicking the Bookmark Name field.

5. You can use the default bookmark name or type a new bookmark name.

6. Press Enter or click OK to accept the bookmark.

   Press Esc or click Cancel to abandon the bookmark.

To select a bookmark in a Help topic

1. Select Help.

2. Select the Bookmark menu.

3. Select the bookmark name from the menu by pressing the number associated with the bookmark name, or by clicking the bookmark name.

To delete a bookmark in a Help topic

1. Select the Help topic.

2. Select the Bookmark menu.

3. Select Define. The Bookmark Define dialog box appears.

4. Press Tab and use the arrow keys to select the bookmark you want to delete. If you are using a mouse, click the Bookmark button.

5. Select Delete by pressing Alt+D or by clicking the Delete button.

To get the Help index for the topic

From the Help window, select Contents by pressing Alt+C or by clicking Contents.

To back up to the last Help text

From the Help window, select Back by pressing Alt+B or by clicking the Back button.

To browse through the Help topics

Some Help files contain Browse buttons (<< or >>) that enable you to move to the previous topic or the next topic, respectively. From the Help window, select << or >> by pressing Alt+< or Alt+>, or by clicking the << or >> buttons.

To search for a Help topic

1. From the Help window, select Search by pressing Alt+S or by clicking the Search button. The Search dialog box appears.

2. Type the topic for which you want to search. As you begin to type text, topics in the next window become selected.

3. When the correct topic is selected, select Show Topics by pressing Alt+S or by clicking the Show Topics button.

4. Choose Select a topic by pressing Alt+T or by clicking the Select a topic list box.

5. Select the correct topic by pressing ↑ and ↓, or by pointing to the topic and clicking the mouse.

6. Select the Go To button by pressing Alt+G, or
    by pointing to the button and clicking the
    mouse.

To search through previously used Help topics

1. From the Help window, choose History by
    pressing Alt+T or by clicking History. The
    History dialog box appears.

2. Use the arrow keys to select the previously
    viewed topic and press Enter. Or double-click
    the previously viewed topic.

To use the Glossary

1. From the Help window choose Glossary by
    pressing Alt+G or by clicking Glossary. The
    Glossary window opens.

2. Scroll through the Glossary by pressing ↑ and
    ↓ or by clicking the up and down scroll arrows
    in the scroll bar.

3. Click the topic.

Icon Selection

General

Purpose

Enables you to select icons so that you can open,
delete, copy, or manipulate a file or application.

To select a Program Group icon with the keyboard

1. Activate the Program Manager.

2. Choose the Window menu by pressing Alt+W.

3. Choose the number associated with the Program Group icon. For example, if the Accessories Program Group icon is number 5 and you want to select the Accessories icon, you press 5.

To select a Program Group icon with the mouse

1. Activate the Program Manager.

2. Point to the correct Program Group icon and click the mouse.

To select a Program Item icon with the keyboard

1. Activate the Program Manager.

2. Select the correct program group by pressing Ctrl+Tab. If the program group is minimized, press Alt+← to open the Control menu, and then press R to select Restore; the group will be restored to a window.

3. Using the arrow keys, highlight the correct Program Item icon.

To select a Program Item icon with the mouse

1. Activate the Program Manager.

2. Point to the correct Program Group icon and click the mouse. If the program group is mini-mized, double-click the Program Group icon.

3. Point to the correct Program Item icon and click the mouse.

Note

Make sure that you select the correct icon. You normally select an icon when you want to copy it, move it, change its properties, or affect it in some other way. Selecting the wrong icon may cause you to affect the wrong icon.

International Options

Purpose

Enables you to operate Windows with the rules for a different country.

To start the following procedures, start the Control Panel from the Main program group. Then choose International from the Settings menu or double-click the International icon.

To change the country

1. From the International Settings dialog box, choose Country by pressing Alt+C or by clicking the Country field.

2. Choose the drop-down list box by pressing Alt+↓ or by clicking the drop-down list arrow.

3. From the list of countries, choose the correct country by using the arrow keys and then pressing Enter. Or use the scroll bars until the correct country is in view, then point to the country and click the mouse.

   When you select the country, all items in the International dialog box change—with the exception of Language and Keyboard Layout.

To change the language

1. From the International Settings dialog box, choose Language by pressing Alt+L or by clicking the Language field.

2. Choose the drop-down list box by pressing Alt+↓ or by clicking the drop-down list arrow.

3. From the list of languages, choose the correct language by using the arrow keys and pressing Enter. Or use the scroll bars until the correct language is in view, then point to the language and click the mouse. Make sure that the language matches all the other country settings.

   For example, if you chose the country Sweden, then you should choose the Swedish language. Windows will prompt you to insert a Windows install disk. Insert the disk and press Enter or click OK.

To change the keyboard layout

1. From the International Settings dialog box, choose Keyboard Layout by pressing Alt+K or by clicking the Keyboard Layout field.

2. Choose the drop-down list box by pressing Alt+↓ or by clicking the drop-down list arrow.

3. From the list of keyboard layouts, choose the correct layout by using the arrow keys and pressing Enter. Or use the scroll bars until the correct layout is in view, then point to the keyboard layout and click the mouse. Make sure that the keyboard layout matches all the other country settings.

   For example, if you chose the country Sweden and the language as Swedish, then choose the Swedish keyboard layout. Windows will prompt you to insert a Windows install disk. Insert the disk and press Enter or click OK.

To change the measurement

1. From the International Settings dialog box, choose Measurement by pressing Alt+M or by clicking the **Measurement** field.

2. Choose the drop-down list box by pressing Alt+↓ or by clicking the drop-down list arrow.

3. From the list of measurements, choose the correct measurement by using the arrow keys and pressing **Enter**. You can choose Metric or English. If you are using a mouse, use the scroll bars until the correct measurement is in view, then point to the measurement and click the mouse.

    Make sure that the measurement matches all the other country settings.

To change the list separator

1. From the International Settings dialog box, choose List Separator by pressing Alt+S or by clicking the **List Separator** field.

2. Type the correct list separator. Make sure that the measurement matches all the other country settings.

To change the date format

1. From the International Settings dialog box, choose Date Format by pressing Alt+D or by clicking the Change button in the Date Format area.

2. Choose the Short Date Format Order by pressing Alt+O, and then press ↑ and ↓ to select

MDY (Month, Day, Year), DMY (Day, Month, Year), or YMD (Year, Month, Day). Or point to either MDY, DMY, or YMD and click the mouse.

3. Choose the Short Date Format **S**eparator by pressing **Alt**+**S** or by clicking the **Short Date Format Separator** field.

4. Type the correct Separator character. Americans use a slash and Europeans use a period as a separator character.

5. Choose Short Date Format **D**ay Leading Zero to begin the day number with a zero. Press **Alt**+**D** or click the **Day Leading Zero** box.

6. Choose Short Date Format **M**onth Leading Zero to begin the month number with a zero. Press **Alt**+**M** or click the **Month Leading Zero** box.

7. Choose Short Date Format **C**entury to specify whether the year shows two digits or four. Press **Alt**+**C** or click the **Century** box.

8. Choose the Long Date Format O**r**der by pressing **Alt**+**R**, and then press ↑ and ↓ to select MDY, DMY, or YMD formats. Or point to either MDY, DMY, or YMD and click the mouse.

9. Press **Tab** to choose whether to display the day name. Press **Alt**+↓ and choose from no day name, a three-letter day name, or full day name. After you make your selection, press **Alt**+↑ . Or click the drop-down list arrow, and click the day name type you want.

10. Press **Tab** to select the punctuation separator. Type the new punctuation, if necessary.

11. Press **Tab** to choose whether to display the month as a number with or without a leading zero, as a name with only three letters, or as the full month name. Press **Alt**+↓, select the correct month option, and press **Alt**+↑. Or click the drop-down list arrow, and click the month option you want.

12. Press Tab to select the next punctuation separator. Type the new punctuation, if necessary.

13. Press Tab to choose whether to display the day number's leading zero. Press Alt+↓. Select no leading zero or a leading zero, and then press Alt+↑. Or click the drop-down list arrow, and click the day number you want.

14. Press Tab to select the next punctuation separator. Type the new punctuation, if necessary.

15. Press Tab to choose whether to display the year with two numbers or with all four numbers. Press Alt+↓, select the correct option, and press Alt+↑. Or click the drop-down list arrow, and click the option you want.

16. Choose OK to accept changes to the International-Date Format by pressing Enter or by clicking OK.

    You can abandon the changes made to the International-Date Format by pressing Esc or by clicking Cancel.

To change the time format

1. From the International Settings dialog box, choose Time Format by pressing Alt+T or by clicking the Change button in the Time Format area.

2. Choose a 12-hour clock by pressing Alt+2 or a 24-hour clock by pressing Alt+4. Or click either 12 hour or 24 hour. If you choose 12 hour, then AM and PM appear next to the appropriate hours.

3. Choose Separator by pressing Alt+S or by clicking the Separator field. Type the separator character you want to use.

4. Choose Leading Zero by pressing Alt+L, and press ↑ and ↓ to select whether you want a

leading zero. Or point to 9:15 and click the mouse if you prefer not to use a leading zero. Point to 09:15 to use a leading zero, and click the mouse.

5. Choose OK to accept changes to the International-Time Format by pressing Enter or by clicking OK.

   To abandon the changes made to the International-Time Format, press Esc or click Cancel.

To change the currency format

1. From the International Settings dialog box, choose Currency Format by pressing Alt+U or by clicking the Change button in the Currency Format area.

2. Choose Symbol Placement by pressing Alt+P or by clicking the Symbol Placement field.

3. Choose one of the four symbol placements by pressing Alt+↓, or by clicking the Symbol Placement drop-down list arrow.

   Use the arrow keys to select the correct symbol placement and press Enter, or click the correct symbol placement.

4. Choose Negative by pressing Alt+N or by clicking the Negative field.

5. Press Alt+↓ or click the Negative drop-down list arrow. Use the arrow keys to select the desired negative format and press Enter. Or point to the desired negative format and click the mouse. You may need to use the scroll bars to reveal other negative options.

6. Choose Symbol by pressing Alt+S or by clicking the Symbol field.

7. Type the desired currency symbol.

8. Choose Decimal Digits by pressing Alt+D or by clicking the Decimal Digits field.

9. Type the number of decimals that should be displayed.

10. Choose OK to accept changes to the International-Currency Format by pressing Enter or by clicking OK.

   To abandon the changes made to the International-Currency Format, press Esc or click Cancel.

To change the number format

1. From the International Settings dialog box, choose Number Format by pressing Alt+N or by clicking the Change button in the Number Format area.

2. Choose 1000 Separator by pressing Alt+S or by clicking the 1000 Separator field.

3. Type the character you want to use for the 1000 separator.

4. Choose Decimal Separator by pressing Alt+D or by clicking the Decimal Separator field.

5. Type the character you want to use for the decimal separator.

6. Choose Decimal Digits by pressing Alt+E or by clicking the Decimal Digits field.

7. Type the number of decimals that should be displayed.

8. Choose Leading Zero by pressing Alt+L, and press → to use a leading zero and ← to choose not to use a leading zero.

   If you are using a mouse, click .7 to not use a leading zero, or click 0.7 to use a leading zero.

9. Choose OK to accept changes to the International-Number Format by pressing Enter or by clicking OK.

To abandon the changes made to the
International-Number Format, press Esc or
click Cancel.

To save all the International options

Choose OK to accept changes to the International-
Number Format by pressing Enter or by clicking OK.

To abandon the changes made to the International-Number Format

Press Esc or click Cancel.

Notes

Use the International options to customize Windows
for a foreign language. Note that when you choose a
country that you normally do not work with, the
keyboard may be different, causing you to type
incorrect information.

The following countries are available: Australia,
Austria, Belgium (Dutch), Belgium (French), Brazil,
Canada (English), Canada (French), Denmark,
Finland, France, Germany, Iceland, Ireland, Italy,
Mexico, Netherlands, New Zealand, Norway,
Portugal, South Korea, Spain, Sweden, Switzerland
(French), Switzerland (German), Switzerland
(Italian), Taiwan, the United Kingdom, the United
States, and Other Country. The default country is
the United States.

Keyboard Modification

Purpose

Enables you to change the key repeat rate of your keyboard. You can, for example, increase or decrease the speed that your cursor moves on-screen.

To change the keyboard speed

1. Start the Control Panel from the Main program group.

2. Choose Keyboard from the Control Panel using the Settings Keyboard command, or point to the Keyboard icon and double-click the mouse.

3. Change Delay Before First Repeat in one of the following ways:

   ■ Press ← and → to move the scroll box to the desired location.

   ■ Click the scroll arrows.

   ■ Point to the scroll box with the mouse, press and hold the left mouse button, drag the scroll box to the desired location, and release the mouse button.

4. Change the key repeat rate in one of the following ways:

   ■ Press ← and → to move the scroll box to the desired location.

   ■ Click the scroll arrows.

   ■ Point to the scroll box with the mouse, press and hold the left mouse button, drag the scroll box to the desired location, and release the mouse button.

5. Test the repeat rate by choosing Test and holding a key on the keyboard.

6. Repeat steps 3–5 until the desired repeat rate is attained.

Notes

When you change the rate of the keyboard, make sure that the rate is not so fast that you cannot keep up with the cursor.

The keyboard stores in a buffer the characters you type so that although the computer is not yet accepting the characters, you can type ahead. If the computer begins beeping as you type, you may need to decrease the key-repeat rate. The beeping means that the buffer is full and the keyboard is not accepting characters.

Link Information

General

Purpose

Inserts information from one document into another document. The inserted information can be automatically updated, or can be changed from inside the second document. This task is based on Paintbrush as the server, or sending application, and Write as the client, or receiving application.

To link an object

1. Start or select the server program. If the object has not been created, then create the object and save it to disk.

2. Select the object from the server program to link to the client document.

3. Choose the Edit menu by pressing Alt+E or by clicking Edit.

4. Choose Copy from the Edit menu by pressing C or by clicking Copy.

5. Start or select the client program. Open the document to link to if it is not already open.

6. Position the cursor in the document where the object should be linked.

7. Choose the Edit menu by pressing Alt+E or by clicking Edit.

8. Choose Paste Link from the Edit menu by pressing L or by clicking Paste Link. Or choose Paste Special, select a Data Type from the Paste Special dialog box, then press Alt+L or click the Paste Link button.

To embed an object

1. Start or select the server program. If the object has not been created, then create the object and save it to disk.

2. Select the object from the server program to link to the client document.

3. Choose the Edit menu by pressing Alt+E or by clicking Edit.

4. Choose Copy from the Edit menu by pressing C or by clicking Copy.

5. Start or select the client program. Open the document to link to if it is not already open.

6. Position the cursor in the document where the object should be linked.

7. Choose the Edit menu by pressing Alt+E or by clicking Edit.

8. Choose Paste from the Edit menu by pressing P or by clicking Paste. Or choose Paste

Special, select a **D**ata Type from the Paste
Special dialog box, then press **Alt+P** or click
the Paste button.

To edit an embedded object

1. Open the program and document that contain
   the embedded object.

2. Select the embedded object.

3. Choose the Edit menu by pressing Alt+E or by
   clicking Edit.

4. Choose Edit Paintbrush Picture Object from
   the Edit menu by pressing O or by clicking
   Edit Paintbrush Picture Object. The server
   program will start with the object to edit.

   > Note: You can double-click the object
   > with the mouse rather than perform
   > steps 3 and 4.

5. Edit the object.

6. Choose the File menu by pressing Alt+F or by
   clicking File.

7. Choose Update from the File menu by pressing
   U or by clicking Update.

8. Choose the File menu by pressing Alt+F or by
   clicking File.

9. Choose Exit & return to *filename* from the File
   menu by pressing X or by clicking Exit &
   return to *filename*.

To update a link

1. Open the program and document that contain
   the linked object.

2. Select the linked object.

3. Choose the Edit menu by pressing Alt+E or by clicking Edit.

4. Choose Links from the Edit menu by pressing K or by clicking Links. The Links dialog box appears.

5. Choose one of the following:

   ■ Links to select the link to work with

   ■ Automatic to automatically update the link

   ■ Manual to update the link manually

   ■ Update Now to update the link

   ■ Cancel Link to remove the link from the document

   ■ Change Link to link to a different file than the one currently selected

   ■ Activate or Edit to change the linked object

   ■ OK to accept the changes; Cancel to abandon changes

Notes

Object Linking and Embedding (OLE) is a powerful feature that is used with Windows 3.1. You can link or embed information of one type into a program of a different type. For example, you can place a graphic drawn with Paintbrush into a Write document. If the Paintbrush graphic is changed, the change also occurs in the Write document. Or you can edit the Paintbrush graphic in the Write document without actually changing the original Paintbrush graphic.

The two programs you link are called the *server* and the *client*. The server is the program that provides the information to link. The client is where the information is linked. If you are linking a graphic from Paintbrush into a Write document, then Paintbrush is the server and Write is the client.

Object linking is different from object embedding. When you link an object, you place an object from the server into a client document. When you change the server object, the change occurs in the client document. When you embed an object, you place a copy of the server object in the client document. Any change to the server object does not occur in the client document. However, by choosing the object in the document, the server program will start and you can edit the object. When you change the object in the document, the change is not made in the original. The change is only reflected in the document.

Maximize Windows

General

Purpose

Enlarges a window so that it takes up the entire screen.

To maximize a window using the keyboard

1. Choose the Control menu by pressing Alt+space bar.

2. Choose Maximize by pressing X. The window will now take up the entire screen.

To maximize a window using the mouse

Click the Maximize button. The Maximize button is the button with the upward-pointing arrow in the upper right corner of the window.

> Note: You can double-click the window's title bar to maximize the window.

Note

When a window is maximized, the Maximize button
in the upper-right corner of the screen changes from
an upward-pointing arrow to two arrows—one
pointing up and the other pointing down. Rather
than maximizing a window, you can change the
window's size to take up the entire screen. A
maximized window cannot be moved on the desktop. Only a non-maximized window can be moved
on the desktop, even if the window has been sized
to take up the entire screen.

Minimize Windows

General

Purpose

Enables you to choose how an application appears.
An application can exist in a window that takes up
the entire screen or a portion of the screen, or as an
icon.

To minimize a window using the keyboard

1. Choose the Control menu by pressing
   Alt+space bar.
2. Choose Minimize by pressing Alt+N. The
   window is reduced to an icon.

To minimize a window using the mouse

Click the Minimize button. The Minimize button is
the button with the downward-pointing arrow in the
upper right corner of the window. The window is
reduced to an icon.

Mouse Customization

Control Panel

Purpose

Changes the sensitivity of the mouse, and enables you to swap the mouse buttons.

To customize the mouse

1. From the Control Panel, choose Mouse by double-clicking the mouse icon. The Mouse dialog box appears.

2. Choose Mouse Tracking Speed by clicking the Mouse Tracking Speed scroll box, pressing and holding the left mouse button, and dragging the scroll box to the desired setting. Release the mouse button. Move the mouse to check the tracking speed. If the speed is not yet correct, repeat this step.

3. Choose Double Click Speed by clicking the Double Click Speed scroll box, pressing and holding the left mouse button, and dragging the scroll box to the desired setting. Release the mouse button. Point to the Test button and double-click the mouse at different speeds. If the speed is not yet correct, repeat this step.

4. Choose Swap Left/Right Buttons to swap the mouse buttons. When the box is checked, the buttons are swapped.

5. Choose Mouse Trails to make the mouse pointer easier to find on an LCD screen.

6. Accept the changes to the mouse by pressing Enter or by clicking OK.

   To abandon the changes, press Esc or click Cancel.

Notes

Mouse sensitivity combines two settings. The first
setting is the mouse tracking speed. The faster the
mouse tracking speed is set, the less space is
needed to move the mouse. However, you trade
accuracy with the mouse for the small desk space
for movement.

The second setting is double-click speed. The faster
this setting, the more rapid you must double-click
the left mouse button.

You also can choose to swap the left and right
mouse buttons. If you are left-handed, you can swap
the mouse buttons so that the mouse button
referred to as the left mouse button can be operated
with your left index finger.

Mouse Trails is a unique feature that makes finding
a mouse pointer easier on an LCD screen. When you
move the mouse with Mouse Trails selected, the
pointer appears to have a shadow.

Move Files

File Manager

Purpose

Enables you to copy a file from one drive and
directory to another drive and directory, deleting
the original file.

*To move a file from one drive to another drive using the
keyboard*

1. Start the File Manager.

2. Place the source disk and destination disk in
   the correct drives. For example, place the

source disk in drive A and the destination disk in drive B. If you are moving to or from a hard disk to a diskette, you only need to place the diskette in the drive.

3. Activate the source disk by pressing Ctrl and the letter associated with the drive. For example, press Ctrl+A to activate drive A.

4. Begin selecting the file or files to move (see *Selecting Files*).

5. Choose the File menu.

6. Choose Move.

> Note: You can press F7 rather than perform steps 5 and 6.

7. When the Move dialog box appears, type the name of the drive to which you want to move in the To text box. If you are moving to a disk in drive B, type B:.

8. Select OK by pressing Enter.

To terminate the move process, press Esc.

_____

To move a file from one drive to another drive using the mouse

1. Start the File Manager.

2. Place the source disk and destination disk in the correct drives. For example, place the source disk in drive A and the destination disk in drive B.

3. Activate the source disk by pointing to the drive icon with the mouse and clicking.

4. Begin selecting the file or files to copy (see *Selecting Files*).

5. Point to the file icon of one of the selected files, and press and hold the Shift key, then press and hold the left mouse button.

6. Drag the Files icon to the destination drive or directory icon. When the Files icon is positioned on the correct destination drive icon, release the mouse button, and release the Shift key.

   The Moving dialog box appears. As the move progresses, you can click Cancel to abandon the move.

Note

Be careful when you move a file. If you move a file to a drive or directory that contains a file by the same name, you may accidentally overwrite the original file with the file you are moving, possibly losing data. To display a confirmation message before a file is replaced, mark the File Replace check box in the Confirmation dialog box. Choose Confirmation from the Options menu for the dialog box.

Moving Program Items

Program Manager

Purpose

Moves a program item to a different program group.

To move a program item using the menus

1. Start the Program Manager.

2. Open the program group that contains the program item you want to move. Select the Window menu by pressing Alt+W, and then press the number associated with the program group. Or point to the program group and double-click the mouse.

3. Select the program item by using ← and →, or by clicking the program item.

4. Choose the File menu.

5. Choose Move. The Move Program Item dialog box appears.

6. Choose To Group by pressing Alt+T or by clicking the To Group field.

7. Select the correct program group by pressing ↑ and ↓, or by clicking the drop-down list arrow, and then clicking the correct program group.

8. To complete the move, press Enter or click OK. Press Esc or click Cancel to abandon the move.

To move a program item using the drag method (mouse only)

1. Start the Program Manager.

2. Open the program group that contains the program item you want to copy by pointing to the program group and double-clicking the mouse.

3. Point to the program item you want to copy, and then press and hold the left mouse button.

4. Drag the program item to the correct program group, and then release the mouse button.

Moving Windows

General

Purpose

Enables you to move each open window so that each window is accessible.

To move a window using the keyboard

1. Select the window you want to move by pressing Ctrl+Esc. The Task List appears.

2. Use ↑ and ↓ to select the correct window and press Enter.

3. Choose the Control menu by pressing Alt+space bar.

4. Choose Move by pressing M.

5. Use the arrow keys to move the window on the screen. When the window is in the desired position, press Enter. Press Esc rather than Enter to return the window to its beginning position.

To move a window using the mouse

1. Point to the window you want to move and click the mouse.

2. Point to the window's title bar, and then press and hold the left mouse button.

3. Move the mouse, and the window moves. When the window is in the desired location, release the mouse button.

Pause a Print Job

Print Manager

Purpose

Pauses a print job. When you are ready, you can resume printing.

To pause a print job

1. Open the Print Manager window if it is not open. Use the Task List by pressing **Ctrl+Esc** or by double-clicking the Print Manager icon.

2. Select the printer you want to pause by using the arrow keys, or by pointing to the printer and clicking the mouse.

3. Choose the **P**ause button by pressing **Alt+P** or by clicking the Pause button. The printer pauses printing, and a hand appears before the printer name.

> Note: To resume printing, follow steps 1 and 2, and then choose the **R**esume button by pressing **Alt+R** or by clicking the Resume button.

Note

If you are working with an application and need maximum processing speed, pause the current print job so that Windows allocates more time to the application. Remember that Windows has not cancelled the print job; printing can be resumed.

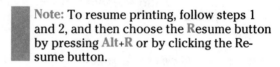

Port Selection

Control Panel

Purpose

Assigns each printer to each port when you have several printers attached to a computer.

To select a port

1. Start the Control Panel from the Main program group.

2. From the Control Panel, choose Printers by choosing the Settings menu, then selecting Printers. Or double-click the Printers icon.

3. Choose Installed Printers by pressing Alt+P, and use the arrow keys to select the correct printer. Or point to the correct printer and click the mouse.

4. Choose Connect by pressing Alt+C or by clicking Connect. The Connect dialog box appears.

5. Choose Ports by pressing Alt+P, and use the arrow keys to select the port to which the printer is attached. Or point to the correct port, and click the mouse.

6. Press Alt+D or click in the Device Not Selected text box. Type the number of seconds Print Manager should continue retrying the printer if it is off-line before a message is displayed.

7. Press Alt+T or click in the Transmission Retry text box. Type the number of seconds Print Manager should wait before a message is displayed telling you the printer cannot accept more information.

8. Select the Fast Printing Direct to Port check box by pressing Alt+F or by clicking in the check box. When this check box is marked, Print Manager works directly with the printer port rather than accessing MS-DOS.

9. Choose OK by pressing Enter or by clicking OK.

   To abandon the selection, press Esc or click Cancel. You return to the Printers dialog box.

10. From the Printers dialog box, choose Close by
    pressing Enter or by clicking Close.

    To abandon the selection, press Esc or click
    Cancel.

Print Files

Purpose

Enables you to print files rather than starting the
application, loading the file, and then issuing the
print command.

To print a file from the menus

1. Start the File Manager.

2. Select the drive that contains the file you want
   to print by pressing Ctrl and the letter corresponding to the drive. For example, press
   Ctrl+C to select drive C. Or point to the drive
   icon and click the mouse.

3. Choose the directory (if one exists) that contains the file you want to print. Use the arrow
   keys to select the directory, or click the
   subdirectory icon with the mouse.

4. Select the file to print by using the arrow keys
   or by pointing to the file and clicking the
   mouse. If you are using the mouse and do not
   see the file, you may have to use the scroll
   bars.

5. Choose the File menu by pressing Alt+F or by
   clicking the File menu.

6. Choose the Print option by pressing P or by
   clicking Print. The Print dialog box appears.

7. If the file name in the Print field is correct, choose OK by pressing Enter or by clicking OK.

   To abandon printing, press Esc or click Cancel. The file will be sent to the Print Manager for printing to the current printer.

To print a file using the Drag method

1. Start the File Manager.

2. Select the drive that contains the file you want to print by clicking the drive icon.

3. Choose the directory (if one exists) that contains the file you want to print by clicking the subdirectory icon.

4. Select the file to print by clicking the file.

5. Drag the file icon to the Print Manager icon, and release the mouse button. The program associated with the data file will start. Choose OK to print the file.

> Note: This procedure works only with files associated with Windows applications.

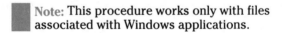

Print Priorities

Print Manager

Purpose

Determines how quickly a document prints. You can switch between low, medium, and high priority.

To set a priority

1. Bring the Print Manager to the foreground.

2. Choose the Options menu by pressing Alt+O or by clicking Options.

3. Choose Low Priority by pressing L or by clicking Low Priority, Medium Priority by pressing M or by clicking Medium Priority, or High Priority by pressing H or by clicking High Priority. A check mark appears next to the priority after you select it.

Note

For times when you need greater processing speed for the application in the foreground, set print priority to low. If you need the document printed quickly, however, set the print priority to high.

Printer Configuration

Control Panel

Purpose

Tells Windows about your printer. You specify paper size, what port the printer is attached to, what fonts the printer supports, and other features of the printer.

To start the following procedures, start the Control Panel from the Main program group. From the Control Panel, choose Printers by choosing Settings and then Printers. Or double-click the Printers icon. Then choose Installed Printers by pressing Alt+P. Use the arrow keys to select the printer to configure. Or point to the Hewlett-Packard printer to configure under Installed Printers and click the mouse.

To configure an HP LaserJet Series II and Series III

1. Choose Connect by pressing Alt+C or by clicking Connect.

2. Choose a port by pressing Alt+P, and then use
   the arrow keys to select the correct port. Or
   point to the correct port under Ports and click
   the mouse.

   > Note: If you select a Com port, then
   > choose the Settings button and configure
   > the serial port.

3. Choose Device Not Selected by pressing Alt+D
   or by clicking the Device Not Selected field.
   Type the number of seconds that Windows
   should wait if a device is not attached or is off-
   line before an error message is displayed. The
   default time is 15, which should be adequate.

4. Choose Transmission Retry by pressing Alt+T
   or by clicking the Transmission Retry field.
   Type the number of seconds that Windows
   should wait before it displays a message about
   the device not receiving characters.

5. Choose Fast Printer Directly To Port by pressing Alt+F or by clicking the Fast Printer Direct
   To Port check box. Use this option for Windows to communicate to the printer, rather
   than going through MS-DOS.

6. Choose OK by pressing Enter or by clicking OK.

7. Choose Setup by pressing Alt+S or by clicking
   Setup.

8. Choose Paper Size by pressing Alt+Z or by
   clicking the Paper Size field. Choose the drop-
   down list box by pressing Alt+↓ or by clicking
   the drop-down list arrow.

9. Choose the correct paper size (normally Letter 8 1/2 x 11 inch) by using ↑ and ↓, and then press Alt+↑. Or point to the correct paper size and click the mouse.

10. Choose Paper Source by pressing Alt+S or by clicking the Paper Source field. Choose the drop-down list box by pressing Alt+↓ or by clicking the drop-down list arrow.

11. Choose the correct paper source (normally Upper Tray) by using ↑ and ↓, and then press Alt+↑. Or point to the correct paper source and click the mouse.

12. Select the Graphics Resolution at which you want to print. Choose 75 dots per inch, 150 dots per inch, or 300 dots per inch by pressing 7, 1, or 3 respectively. Or point to one of the Graphics Resolutions and click the mouse.

13. Choose Copies by pressing Alt+C or by clicking the Copies field. Type the number of copies that should be printed each time you choose to print. Normally, this value will be 1; however, typing 2 here will save you from running to the copier if you normally copy all documents.

14. Choose Memory by pressing Alt+M or by clicking the Memory field. Choose the drop-down list box by pressing Alt+↓ or by clicking the drop-down list arrow.

15. Choose the correct amount of memory by using ↑ and ↓, and then press Alt+↑. Or point to the correct amount of memory and click the mouse.

16. Select the correct paper orientation. Select to print Portrait or Landscape by pressing Alt+R or Alt+L, or by clicking the appropriate option.

17. You can choose up to two Cartridges to plug into the printer. Using the keyboard, press Alt+T, and use ↑ and ↓ to highlight a cartridge.

Press the space bar to select the cartridge.
Repeat this procedure to select the second
cartridge.

Or

Use the scroll bars to display the cartridges.
Point to the correct cartridge and click the
mouse. Point to the second cartridge and click
the mouse again.

18. There are special settings that you may
    choose for the printer. Choose the Options
    button by pressing Alt+O or by clicking
    Options. The options are as follows:

Option	Description
Gray Scale	Select how the printer should handle graphics. You may select from Photographic Images, Line Art Images, or HP ScanJet Images.
None	No duplex printing.
Long Edge	Duplex printing using portrait orientation.
Short Edge	Duplex printing using landscape orientation.
Upper	Use the upper output bin for paper.
Lower	Use the lower output bin for paper.
Print TrueType as Graphics	Treat TrueType as bit-mapped graphics.
Job Separation	Separate each print job by offsetting the documents (HP III SI only).

19. Choose OK to complete the Options dialog box by pressing Enter or by clicking OK.

    To abandon the configuration, press Esc or click Cancel. You return to the Printers-Configure dialog box.

20. Choose OK to complete configuring the printer by pressing Enter or by clicking OK.

    To abandon the configuration, press Esc or click Cancel. You return to the Printers dialog box.

21. Press Alt+E or click the Set as Default Printer button to make this printer the default Windows printer.

22. Choose Use Print Manager if the device should receive information from Windows' Print Manager, or if the printer will receive information directly from the application. Choose Use Print Manager by pressing Alt+U or by clicking Use Print Manager.

23. To save the changes, press Enter or click the Close button.

To configure a Postscript printer

1. Choose Connect by pressing Alt+C or by clicking Connect.

2. Choose a port by pressing Alt+P, and then use the arrow keys to select the correct port. Or point to the correct port under Ports and click the mouse.

   Note: If you select a Com port, then choose the Settings button and configure the serial port.

3. Choose Device Not Selected by pressing Alt+D or by clicking the Device Not Selected field.

Type the number of seconds that Windows
should wait if a device is not attached or is off-
line before an error message is displayed. The
default time is 15, which should be adequate.

4. Choose Transmission Retry by pressing Alt+T
   or by clicking the Transmission Retry field.
   Type the number of seconds that Windows
   should wait before it displays a message about
   the device not receiving characters.

5. Choose Fast Printer Direct To Port by pressing
   Alt+F or by clicking the Fast Printer Direct To
   Port check box. Use this option for Windows
   to communicate to the printer, rather than
   going through MS-DOS.

6. Choose OK by pressing Enter or by clicking OK.

7. Choose Setup by pressing Alt+S or by clicking
   Setup.

8. Choose Paper Source by pressing Alt+S or by
   clicking the Paper Source field. Choose the
   drop-down list box by pressing Alt+↓ or by
   clicking the drop-down list arrow.

9. Choose the correct paper source (normally
   Upper Tray) by using ↑ and ↓, and then press
   Alt+↑. Or point to the correct paper source
   and click the mouse.

10. Choose Paper Size by pressing Alt+Z or by
    clicking the Paper Size field. Choose the drop-
    down list box by pressing Alt+↓ or by clicking
    the drop-down list arrow.

11. Choose the correct paper size (normally Letter
    8 1/2 x 11 inch) by using ↑ and ↓, and then
    press Alt+↑. Or point to the correct paper size
    and click the mouse.

12. Choose Copies by pressing Alt+C or by click-
    ing the Copies field. Type the number of
    copies that should be printed each time you

choose to print. Normally, this value will be 1; however, typing 2 here will save you from running to the copier if you normally copy all documents.

13. Select the correct paper orientation. Select to print Portrait or Landscape by pressing Alt+R or Alt+L, or by clicking the appropriate option.

14. There are special settings you may choose for the printer. Choose the Options button by pressing Alt+O or by clicking Options. The options are as follows:

Option	Description
Printer	Send output to the printer.
Encapsulated Postscript File	Send output to a file rather than a printer. You must name the file in the Name text box.
Default	Use the default margins.
None	Use no margins.
Scaling	Reduce or increase the scaling of the output.
Send Header with Each Job	Send a Postscript header with each print job, rather than just once. Define the header in the Send Header dialog box.

15. Choose OK to complete the Options dialog box by pressing Enter or by clicking OK.

To abandon the configuration, press Esc or click Cancel. You return to the Printers dialog box.

16. Choose OK to complete configuring the printer by pressing Enter or by clicking OK.

To abandon the configuration, press Esc or click Cancel. You return to the Printers dialog box.

17. Press Alt+E or click the Set as Default Printer button to make this printer the default Windows printer.

18. Choose Use Print Manager if the device should receive information from Windows' Print Manager, or if the printer will receive information directly from the application. Choose Use Print Manager by pressing Alt+U or by clicking Use Print Manager.

19. To save changes, press Enter or click the Close button.

Program Properties

Program Manager

Purpose

Specifies the program item name, file name, and location on the disk. The program properties also contain a picture of the icon.

To change a program's properties

1. Start the File Manager.

2. Open the program group that contains the program item whose properties you want to change. Choose the Window menu, and then choose the number associated with the program group.

3. Select the program item that contains the properties you want to change by using the arrow keys, or by pointing to the program item and clicking the mouse.

4. Choose the File menu by pressing Alt+F or by clicking File.

5. Choose the Properties option by pressing P or by clicking Properties. The Program Item Properties dialog box appears.

6. Press Alt+D or click the Description field. Type the name that will appear under the icon. Suppose, for example, that you want to change the current description from EXCEL to EXCEL AMORT. You might type EXCEL AMORT for the description.

7. Press Alt+C or click Command Line. Type the name of the file that starts the program. You may have to include the path pointing to the file.

   Suppose that you want to load an Excel worksheet called AMORT.XLS rather than just EXCEL. AMORT.XLS resides in the C:\SHEETS directory. Type C:\SHEETS\AMORT.XLS in the Command Line text box.

   If you do not know the name of the file, press Alt+B or click the Browse button. The Browse dialog box lists files that you can choose.

8. Press Alt+W or click Working Directory. Type the name of the directory where the program files are located. If you leave this area blank, then the default is the location of the starting program.

9. Press Alt+S or click Shortcut Key. Type a key combination to use to quickly select the program when it is open on the desktop.

10. Select Run Minimized to start the program as an icon rather than a Window.

11. To change the icon, press Alt+I or click the Change Icon button. The Select Icon dialog box appears.

12. Press Alt+F or click the File Name field. Type PROGMAN.EXE or MORICONS.DLL.

13. Choose the icon to use in the Current Icon selection box. Change to the desired icon and press Enter or click OK.

14. To finish changing the program item, choose OK by pressing Enter or by clicking OK.

    To cancel the operation, press Esc or click Cancel.

Remove/Add Windows Files

See *Add/Remove Windows Files*.

Rename Files

File Manager

Purpose

Enables you to assign a new file name. When you rename a file, you cannot use a name that already exists.

To rename a file

1. Start the File Manager.

2. From the File Manager, select the drive containing the file or files you want to rename by pressing Ctrl and the letter of the drive. For example, press Ctrl+C for drive C. Or point to the disk drive icon and click the mouse.

3. From the Directory Tree, select the subdirectory that contains the file or files you want to rename. Use the arrow keys to select the subdirectory, or click the subdirectory.

4. Select the file to rename (see *Selecting Files*).

5. Choose the File menu by pressing Alt+F or by clicking File.

6. Choose Rename by pressing N or by clicking Rename.

7. When the Rename dialog box appears, type the new name in the To field.

8. Choose Rename by pressing Enter or by clicking OK. To abandon the process, press Esc or click Cancel.

Restore Windows

General

Purpose

Changes an icon or a window to its previous size.

To restore a window from an icon

1. Select the icon to restore by pressing Alt+Esc, or by pointing to the icon and clicking the mouse.

2. If you selected the icon using the keyboard, press Alt+space bar to choose the Control menu. If you selected the icon using the mouse, the Control menu is already open.

3. Choose Restore by pressing R or by clicking Restore.

To restore a window to its previous size

1. Select the window to restore by pressing Alt+Esc, or by pointing to the window and clicking the mouse.

2. Choose the Control menu by pressing
   Alt+space bar, or by clicking the Control
   menu.

3. Choose Restore by pressing R or by clicking
   Restore.

Resume a Print Job

Print Manager

Purpose

Resumes a print job that has been paused.

To resume a print job

1. Open the Print Manager window if it is not
   open by using the Task List or by double-
   clicking the Print Manager icon with the
   mouse.

2. Select the printer you want to resume printing
   by using the arrow keys or by pointing to the
   printer and clicking the mouse.

3. Choose the Resume button by pressing Alt+R
   or by clicking Resume. The printer resumes
   printing, and the hand that appeared in front
   of the printer name disappears.

Note

If you are working with an application and need
maximum processing speed, you can pause the
current print job so that Windows allocates more
time to the application. When you are ready, you
can resume printing.

Run Files

Program Manager or File Manager

Purpose

Enables you to start applications from the Program Manager or the File Manager.

To run a program using menu commands

1. Select the Program Manager or start the File Manager.

2. Choose the File menu by pressing Alt+F or by clicking File.

3. Choose Run by pressing R or by clicking Run.

4. When the Run dialog box appears, type in the Command Line field the program you want to run.

   Select Run Minimized if the application should shrink to an icon.

5. Choose OK by pressing Enter or by clicking OK.

   To abandon Run, press Esc or click Cancel.

To run a program using the mouse

1. Select the Program Manager or start the File Manager.

2. From the File Manager, click the drive containing the file you want to run.

3. From the Directory Tree, click the subdirectory that contains the file you want to run.

4. Double-click the file name to run.

Search for Files

File Manager

Purpose

Enables you to find a file when you do not remember in what directory the file is located.

To find a file

1. Start the File Manager.

2. Choose the File menu by pressing Alt+F or by clicking File.

3. Choose Search by pressing H or by clicking Search. The Search dialog box appears.

4. Choose Search For by pressing Alt+S or by clicking the Search For field.

5. Type the search string, using wild-card characters if desired.

   Suppose, for example, that you are searching for LETTER.TXT. Type LETTER.TXT. If you are searching for all files with the NTE extension, type *.NTE.

6. Choose the Start From text box by pressing Alt+F or by clicking in the Start From text box.

7. Type the name of the directory from which to start the search. To search all of drive C, type C:\.

8. Choose Search All Subdirectories by pressing Alt+E or by clicking the Search All Subdirectories check box.

9. To begin searching, choose OK by pressing Enter or by clicking OK.

   To abandon the search, press Esc or click Cancel.

10. If files are found, the Search Results window appears. You may act upon (activate, copy, or delete, for example) the files shown.

Notes

When searching for files, you may search through a directory branch or search through the entire disk.

All files that are found are displayed in a window with the entire path pointing to the file. You can open any of the files in the window, starting an associated application.

Selecting Files

File Manager

Purpose

Highlights a file or group of files to act upon.

To select a single file using the keyboard

1. Start the File Manager from the Main program group.

2. From the Directory Tree, select the directory that contains the file you want to act on. Use the arrow keys to select the correct directory.

3. Press Tab to change from the directory window to the files window.

4. Highlight the correct file, using the arrow keys and space bar.

To select a single file using the mouse

1. Start the File Manager from the Main program group.

2. From the Directory Tree, point to the directory that contains the file or files to select and click the mouse.

3. Point to the correct file and click the mouse to select the file.

To select a contiguous group of files using the keyboard

1. Start the File Manager from the Main program group.

2. From the Directory Tree, select the directory that contains the file you want to act on. Use the arrow keys to select the correct directory.

3. Press Tab to change from the directory window to the files window.

4. Highlight the correct file, using the arrow keys and space bar.

5. Press and hold the Shift key, then use the arrow keys to begin highlighting files.

   The highlight begins expanding over the files. Use ↑ and ↓ to highlight the next or previous file in a column, or ← and → to highlight columns of files. When all necessary files have been selected, release the keys.

To select a contiguous group of files using the mouse

1. Start the File Manager from the Main program group.

2. From the Directory Tree, point to the directory that contains the file or files to select and click the mouse.

3. Point to the first file to select and click the mouse.

4. Point to the last file to select, press and hold the Shift key, then click the mouse. Release the Shift key.

To select a noncontiguous group of files using the keyboard

1. Start the File Manager from the Main program group.

2. From the Directory Tree, select the directory that contains the file you want to act on. Use the arrow keys to select the correct directory.

3. Press Tab to change from the directory window to the files window.

4. Highlight the first file, using the arrow keys.

5. Press Shift+F8. The selection outline begins blinking.

6. Using the arrow keys, move the selection outline to the next file to select. Press the space bar. Repeat this step to continue selecting files.

To select a noncontiguous group of files using the mouse

1. Start the File Manager from the Main program group.

2. From the Directory Tree, point to the directory that contains the file or files to select and click the mouse.

3. Point to the first file to select and click the mouse.

4. Point to the next file to select, press and hold the Ctrl key, then click the mouse. Release the Ctrl key. Repeat this step to continue selecting files.

Selecting the Default Printer

Print Manager

Purpose

Assigns the printer that Windows will use as the default printer.

To assign the default printer

1. Start the Print Manager. If it is already running on the desktop, make the Print Manager the active application by pressing Alt+Tab until the Print Manager is the selected application. Or double-click the Print Manager icon.

2. Choose the Options menu by pressing Alt+O or by clicking Options.

3. Choose Printer Setup by pressing P or by clicking Printer Setup. The Printers dialog box appears.

4. Choose the printer in the Installed Printers list box by pressing Alt+P and using the arrow keys to select the correct printer, or by clicking the printer.

5. Press Alt+E or click Set As Default Printer to set the selected printer as the default printer.

6. Press Enter or click Close to accept the change.

Notes

If you have installed only one printer driver for Windows, that printer is the default printer. However, if you have installed more than one printer driver, you can choose which printer is the default printer.

The default printer is the printer to which Windows will send information when you select to print a file. Select the printer you use most often as the default printer.

Sizing Windows

General

Purpose

Changes the size of a window.

To size a window using the keyboard

1. Activate the window to size using the Task List.

2. Press Alt+space bar to activate the window's Control menu.

3. Choose Size by pressing S.

4. Press the arrow key that points to the side of the window to begin sizing. Pressing the up arrow begins sizing the top of the window. The right arrow begins sizing the right side of the window. The left arrow begins sizing the left side of the window. The down arrow begins sizing the bottom of the window.

5. As an option, after you have selected the side to begin sizing, you can select a corner to begin sizing. After you press the up arrow or the down arrow, pressing the right or left arrow enables you to begin sizing the right or left corner of the side you selected. If you originally pressed the right- or left-arrow key to begin sizing the right or left side of the window, the up- or down-arrow key enables you to begin sizing the top or bottom corner of the respective side.

6. Use the arrow keys to change the size of the window. You will see the outline of the window change, reflecting the size of the window.

7. Press Enter to quit sizing the window.

To size a window using the mouse

1. Activate the window you want to size by pointing to it and clicking the mouse. If the window is hidden by another window, either move the window or access the Task List.

2. Point to the side or corner of the window to begin sizing. If you point to a side of the window, the mouse arrow will change to a double-headed arrow that points left and right or up and down. If you point to a corner of the window, the mouse arrow will change to a double-headed arrow that points diagonally.

3. When the arrow has changed to a double-headed arrow, press and hold the mouse button.

4. Move the mouse. You will see the outline of the window change, reflecting the size of the window. When the window is the desired size, release the mouse button.

Sound and Video Drivers

Control Panel

Purpose

Enables you to add, delete, or set up drivers for sound and video.

To start the following procedures, start the Control Panel from the Main program group. Then choose

Drivers from the Control Panel by selecting Drivers
with the arrow keys and pressing Enter, or by
double-clicking the Drivers icon.

To add a new driver

1. From the Drivers dialog box, choose the Add
   button by pressing Tab until Add is selected
   and pressing Enter. You also can press Alt+A
   or click the Add button.

2. Select the driver listed in the List of drivers
   list box. If no correct driver is listed, select
   Unlisted or Updated Driver.

3. Choose OK by pressing Enter or by clicking
   OK. Windows will prompt you to insert the
   correct disk in a disk drive. To cancel, press
   Esc or click Cancel.

4. Place the disk containing the driver in the
   drive requested.

5. Choose OK by pressing Enter or by clicking
   OK. The driver will be copied into Windows.

6. Choose the Close button by pressing Tab until
   Close is selected, then press Enter. Or click
   the Close button.

To remove an existing driver

1. From the Drivers dialog box, press Alt+I to
   select the Installed Drivers list box. Use the
   arrow keys to select the driver to remove. Or
   click the driver to remove in the Installed Drivers list box.

2. Choose the Remove button by pressing Tab
   until Remove is selected, then press Enter.
   You also can press Alt+R or click the Remove
   button.

3. Choose the Close button by pressing Tab until Close is selected, then press Enter. Or click the Close button.

To set up an existing driver

1. From the Drivers dialog box, press Alt+I to select the Installed Drivers list box. Use the arrow keys to select the driver to set up. Or click the driver to set up in the Installed Drivers list box.

2. Choose the Setup button by pressing Tab until Setup is selected, then press Enter. Or click the Setup button.

3. Make all changes according to the driver that you are setting up.

4. Choose the Close button by pressing Tab until Close is selected, then press Enter. Or click the Close button.

Note

Windows 3.1 is capable of multimedia—displaying video and sound. Using the Drivers section of the Control Panel, you can add, remove, or set up drivers. Windows comes with several drivers. For example, there are drivers for the AdLib sound boards, the SoundBlaster sound boards, and MIDI equipment. Some equipment you purchase may come with drivers. In this case, you should add the drivers that accompany the equipment. Make sure, however, that the drivers are compatible with Windows 3.1.

Standard Mode

PIF Editor

Purpose

Allocates computer resources for the non-Windows program to use. To use Standard DOS applications with Windows, you must create a Program Information File (PIF).

To select the Standard mode using the keyboard or mouse

1. Start the PIF Editor accessory.

2. Select Mode.

3. If there is not a check mark next to Standard, then select Standard.

   If you are changing modes, a dialog box appears and asks if you are sure that you want to switch. Select OK.

To enter information for the Standard mode (using Lotus 1-2-3 Release 2.2 as an example)

1. Enter the Program Filename. You must enter the entire name used to start the program, including the path, root name, and extension. An example is C:\123\LOTUS.COM.

2. Enter the Window Title that appears at the top of the window. Enter, for example, Lotus Access System.

3. Enter any Optional Parameters. These parameters, such as switches, are used by the program when it starts. Lotus 1-2-3 allows you to supply a different configuration, called a SET file. You can enter, for example, COLOR.SET, if this is the name of a valid configuration file.

4. Enter the Start-up Directory that the program
   will use. Some programs store their data in
   the current directory. In this example, type
   C:\123.

5. Select the Correct Video Mode. If the program
   displays only text, select Text. If the program
   displays graphics only or text and graphics,
   select Graphics/Multiple Text.

6. Enter the memory required to run the program
   in the Memory Requirements: KB Required
   field. If the minimum memory required to run
   the program is 256K, then type 256.

7. Enter the XMS Memory (extended memory)
   requirements and limit. If the program uses
   XMS memory, enter the KB Required. To prevent the program from using all XMS memory,
   enter the KB Limit.

8. If the program controls one of the communications ports or the keyboard, then select COM1,
   COM2, COM3, COM4, or Keyboard.

9. To keep from exchanging data between this
   program and another, select No Screen Ex-
   change. Selecting this option also frees some
   memory.

10. Select Prevent Program Switch to keep this
    program from being switched away (and an-
    other program from becoming the current
    program). This procedure is important for
    communications that must be active at all
    times.

11. Select Close Window on Exit to close the win-
    dow when you quit the program.

12. Select the No Screen Save check box if the
    program does not redraw the entire screen, or
    does not contain a command to redraw the
    screen.

    When this check box is selected, Windows sets
    aside memory to keep a copy of the screen

when you switch away from the program. When you return to the program, Windows replaces the screen. If you do not select this option, the screen will not restore correctly when switching away from and back to the program. Edit the PIF and select the check box.

13. Select Reserve Shortcut Keys to enable the program to use the key combinations Alt+Tab, Alt+Esc, Ctrl+Esc, PrtSc, or Alt+PrtSc. Normally, Windows uses these keys. If the program needs the keys, select each key combination the program uses, and Windows will ignore it.

To save the PIF file using the keyboard or mouse

1. Select the File menu.

2. Select Save As.

3. Select File Name and type the name of the PIF, following the standard DOS convention of no more than eight characters per name.

   Make sure that the drive and directory are where you want to save the new PIF file.

4. Press Enter or click OK to complete the save.

Note

When you use Windows Standard mode, you can open many non-Windows applications at a time. You can switch from application to application. The PIF file contains necessary information for Windows to start a non-Windows application.

Starting Programs

Program Manager

Purpose

Activates applications in memory.

To start an application using the keyboard

1. Open the Program Manager.

2. Open the Program Group window that contains the application icon you want to start. You can open the Program Group window by pressing Alt+W to open the Window menu, and then pressing the number associated with the Program Group name from the Window menu.

3. Using the arrow keys, select the correct Program Item icon.

4. Press Enter to start the application. Or press Alt+F to choose the File menu, and then press O to Open the application.

To start an application using the mouse

1. Open the Program Manager.

2. Open the Program Group window that contains the application icon you want to start. You can open the Program Group window by pointing to the open window and clicking the mouse. If the Program Group is in icon form, point to the Program Group icon and double-click.

3. Point to the Program Item icon and double-click.

Notes

Rather than typing the name of the file that starts the application at the DOS prompt, each application in Windows is represented by a Program Item icon. An icon is a graphic symbol that in some way represents the type of application it will start. For example, the Calculator accessory icon looks like a small calculator.

Windows applications have icons that are displayed in the Program Manager. If the application is a DOS application, however, you should create a Program Information File (PIF) and create a program item that points to the PIF. The icon will look like a computer screen with the word DOS on the screen, representing a DOS application. You can change the icon of the DOS application to represent the type of application that it is. For example, one of the icons is a computer screen with a telephone on the screen. This may represent a communications program. By selecting the icon, you easily can start the application.

Switching Applications

General

Purpose

Moves different applications into the foreground.

To switch applications using the keyboard

Press Ctrl+Esc.

You move from application to application in a round-robin fashion. Even minimized applications (ones displayed as icons) appear in the cycle. When

a minimized application is the foreground application, the name appears highlighted under the icon.
You can press Alt+space bar to choose the Control
menu, and then choose to restore or maximize the
icon.

To switch applications using the Task List

1. Press Ctrl+Esc. Or point to the Desktop and
   double-click the mouse. The Task List appears.

2. Use the arrow keys to select the application
   you want to make current. If you are using a
   mouse, point to the application and click.

3. Choose Switch To by pressing Alt+S or by
   clicking the Switch To button. Or point to the
   application you want to switch to in the list
   and double-click the mouse. The application
   becomes active.

To switch applications using the mouse

Point to the application and click the mouse. If other
windows are in the way, you may have to move
them. If the application you want to make current is
displayed as an icon, point to the icon and double-
click.

Note

When you have more than one application open,
only one application is in the foreground. You can
switch between applications. You may use the
mouse, keyboard, or call the Task List to switch
applications. Normally, you will use the mouse or
the keyboard. However, if you have several applications open, or if you seem to have lost the application you want to switch to, use the Task List. The
Task List lists all open windows from which you can
choose.

Task List

Purpose

Switches among applications, closes applications, and arranges windows and icons.

To start the following procedures, press **Ctrl**+**Esc**, or point to the Desktop and double-click the mouse. The Task List appears.

To switch to an application

1. Use the arrow keys to select the application you want to make the current application. Or point to the application and click the mouse.

2. Choose **S**witch To by pressing **Alt**+**S** or by clicking the Switch To button. (If you are using a mouse, you can point to the application to switch to in the list and double-click.) The application becomes active.

To close an application

1. Use the arrow keys to select the application you want to close. Or point to the application and click the mouse.

2. Choose **E**nd Task by pressing **Alt**+**E** or by clicking the End Task button.

To arrange all open windows so that each window is in view and the same size (tiling)

Choose **T**ile by pressing **Alt**+**T** or by clicking the Tile button.

To arrange all open windows so that each window is stacked and the same size (cascading)

Choose Cascade by pressing Alt+C or by clicking the Cascade button.

To arrange all icons at the bottom of the screen

Choose Arrange Icons by pressing Alt+A or by clicking the Arrange Icons button.

Note

You can use the Task List to switch among active applications, whether they are windows or icons. If you switch to an icon, it is placed as the foreground application and restored to a window. The Task List not only enables you to bring an application to the foreground, but also enables you to manage tasks, such as closing an application, and arrange icons and windows to make tasks easier to find.

View a Directory

File Manager

Purpose

Opens a directory window to view the files contained in the directory.

To view a directory

1. Start the File Manager.

2. Choose the drive that contains the directory to view by pressing Ctrl and the letter associated with the drive. For example, to make drive C

the current drive, press Ctrl+C. Or point to the drive icon at the top of the Directory Tree window and click the mouse.

3. Use the arrow keys to highlight the directory you want to view. Use + and – to expand and contract directories that contain sub-directories. Or point to the directory you want to view and click the mouse. Double-click a directory to view any subdirectories contained in the directory.

Note

The Directory Tree window displays all sub-directories for a disk drive. Files are displayed in the Files window adjacent to the Directory window.

Viewing Files

File Manager

Purpose

Displays file names only or file names and details. Sorts file names.

To start the following procedures, start the File Manager from the Main program group. Then choose the View menu by pressing Alt+V or by clicking View.

To display file names only

Choose Name by pressing N or by clicking Name. A check mark by the option means that only file names will be displayed.

To display file names and all details

Choose All File Details by pressing A or by clicking All File Details. A check mark by the option means that the file name and all details, such as date and time last modified, will be displayed.

To display file names and partial details

1. Choose Partial Details by pressing P or by clicking Partial Details. The Partial Details dialog box appears.

2. Click the Size check box or press S to display file sizes.

3. Click the Last Modification Date check box or press M to display file dates.

4. Click the Last Modification Time check box or press T to display file times.

5. Click the File Attributes check box or press F to display file attributes.

6. Press Enter or click OK to accept the file details to display. A check mark by the option Partial Details means that the file name and only the details you have selected will be displayed.

To display a sorted file list

Choose one of the following:

- Sort by Name by pressing S or by clicking Sort by Name. Files will be sorted by their names.

- Sort by Type from the View menu by pressing B or by clicking Sort by Type. Files will be sorted by their extensions.

■ Sort by Size from the View menu by pressing Z or by clicking Sort by Size. Files will be sorted by their sizes.

■ Sort by Date from the View menu by pressing D or by clicking Sort by Date. Files will be sorted by their dates.

A check mark appears by the selected Sort option.

To display by file types

1. Choose By File Type by pressing T or by clicking By File Type. The By File Type dialog box appears.

2. Click the Directories check box or press D to display directories in the file list.

3. Click the Programs check box or press P to display programs in the file list.

4. Click the Documents check box or press M to display associated files.

5. Click the Other Files check box or press O to display other files.

6. Press Enter or click OK to accept the changes to the file types display.

To cancel, press Esc or click Cancel.

To display a specific group of files

1. Choose By File Type by pressing T or by clicking By File Type. The By File Type dialog box appears.

2. Press Alt+N or double-click the Name text box to select the Name text box.

3. Type the file specification of the group of files to display, using any legal characters and wild cards. For example, to display all files with, at most, four characters in the root name and the extension of PRG, type ????.PRG.

4. You can specify the types of files that match your specified file name. Select the Directories check box to display directories; the Program check box to display files with the extensions EXE, COM, PIF, or BAT; the Documents check box to display associated files; and the Other Files check box to display any other types of files.

5. Select the Show Hidden/System Files option to display DOS files or other files that normally do not appear in a directory. Exercise care, however. These files are hidden so that they will not be altered or deleted.

6. Press Enter or click OK to accept the changes to the file types display.

   To cancel, press Esc or click Cancel.

Notes

The File Manager displays files contained in each directory. From the View menu, you can select to show just the file name or details about the file. You may sort the names in different ways. You may sort by the file's root name or extension. You also can sort by the file's size or date of last modification. You also can specify to only show certain files. For example, you can choose to include in the list of files only those files with the EXE extension. Or, you can choose to only show program files—that is, files with the extension COM, EXE, BAT, and PIF.

You may be alarmed if you display the files in a directory and do not see a file that you know should be in the directory. However, remember that you may have limited the files for viewing. Change the file type so that you are displaying all files.

Window Selection

General

See *Switching Applications*.

INDEX

Computer Books from Que Mean PC Performance!

Spreadsheets

1-2-3 Beyond the Basics	$24.95
1-2-3 Database Techniques	$29.95
1-2-3 for DOS Release 2.3 Quick Reference	$ 9.95
1-2-3 for DOS Release 2.3 QuickStart	$19.95
1-2-3 for Windows Quick Reference	$ 9.95
1-2-3 for Windows QuickStart	$19.95
1-2-3 Graphics Techniques	$24.95
1-2-3 Macro Library, 3rd Edition	$39.95
1-2-3 Release 2.2 PC Tutor	$39.95
1-2-3 Release 2.2 QueCards	$19.95
1-2-3 Release 2.2 Workbook and Disk	$29.95
1-2-3 Release 3 Workbook and Disk	$29.95
1-2-3 Release 3.1 Quick Reference	$ 8.95
1-2-3 Release 3.1 + QuickStart, 2nd Edition	$19.95
Excel for Windows Quick Reference	$ 9.95
Quattro Pro Quick Reference	$ 8.95
Quattro Pro 3 QuickStart	$19.95
Using 1-2-3/G	$29.95
Using 1-2-3 for DOS Release 2.3, Special Edition	$29.95
Using 1-2-3 for Windows	$29.95
Using 1-2-3 Release 3.1, + 2nd Edition	$29.95
Using Excel 3 for Windows, Special Edition	$29.95
Using Quattro Pro 3, Special Edition	$24.95
Using SuperCalc5, 2nd Edition	$29.95

Databases

dBASE III Plus Handbook, 2nd Edition	$24.95
dBASE IV PC Tutor	$29.95
dBASE IV Programming Techniques	$29.95
dBASE IV Quick Reference	$ 8.95
dBASE IV 1.1 QuickStart	$19.95
dBASE IV Workbook and Disk	$29.95
Que's Using FoxPro	$29.95
Using Clipper, 2nd Edition	$29.95
Using DataEase	$24.95
Using dBASE IV	$29.95
Using ORACLE	$29.95
Using Paradox 3	$24.95
Using PC-File	$24.95
Using R:BASE	$29.95

Business Applications

Allways Quick Reference	$ 8.95
Introduction to Business Software	$14.95
Introduction to Personal Computers	$19.95
Norton Utilities Quick Reference	$ 8.95
PC Tools Quick Reference, 2nd Edition	$ 8.95
Q&A Quick Reference	$ 8.95
Que's Computer User's Dictionary, 2nd Edition	$10.95
Que's Using Enable	$29.95
Que's Wizard Book	$12.95
Quicken Quick Reference	$ 8.95
SmartWare Tips, Tricks, and Traps, 2nd Edition	$26.95
Using DacEasy, 2nd Edition	$24.95
Using Managing Your Money, 2nd Edition	$19.95
Using Microsoft Works: IBM Version	$22.95
Using Norton Utilities	$24.95
Using PC Tools Deluxe	$24.95
Using Peachtree	$27.95
Using PROCOMM PLUS, 2nd Edition	$24.95
Using Q&A 4	$27.95
Using Quicken: IBM Version, 2nd Edition	$19.95
Using SmartWare II	$29.95
Using Symphony, Special Edition	$29.95
Using TimeLine	$24.95
Using TimeSlips	$24.95

CAD

AutoCAD Quick Reference	$ 8.95
Que's Using Generic CADD	$29.95
Using AutoCAD, 3rd Edition	$29.95
Using Generic CADD	$24.95

Word Processing

Microsoft Word Quick Reference	$ 9.95
Using LetterPerfect	$22.95
Using Microsoft Word 5.5: IBM Version, 2nd Edition	$24.95
Using MultiMate	$24.95
Using PC-Write	$22.95
Using Professional Write	$22.95
Using Word for Windows	$24.95
Using WordPerfect 5	$27.95
Using WordPerfect 5.1, Special Edition	$27.95
Using WordStar, 3rd Edition	$27.95
WordPerfect PC Tutor	$39.95
WordPerfect Power Pack	$39.95
WordPerfect 5 Workbook and Disk	$29.95
WordPerfect 5.1 QueCards	$19.95
WordPerfect 5.1 Quick Reference	$ 8.95
WordPerfect 5.1 QuickStart	$19.95
WordPerfect 5.1 Tips, Tricks, and Traps	$24.95
WordPerfect 5.1 Workbook and Disk	$29.95

Hardware/Systems

DOS Tips, Tricks, and Traps	$24.95
DOS Workbook and Disk, 2nd Edition	$29.95
Fastback Quick Reference	$ 8.95
Hard Disk Quick Reference	$ 8.95
MS-DOS PC Tutor	$39.95
MS-DOS 5 Quick Reference	$ 9.95
MS-DOS 5 QuickStart, 2nd Edition	$19.95
MS-DOS 5 User's Guide, Special Edition	$29.95
Networking Personal Computers, 3rd Edition	$24.95
Understanding UNIX: A Conceptual Guide, 2nd Edition	$21.95
Upgrading and Repairing PCs	$29.95
Using Microsoft Windows 3, 2nd Edition	$24.95
Using MS-DOS 5	$24.95
Using Novell NetWare	$29.95
Using OS/2	$29.95
Using PC DOS, 3rd Edition	$27.95
Using Prodigy	$19.95
Using UNIX	$29.95
Using Your Hard Disk	$29.95
Windows 3 Quick Reference	$ 8.95

Desktop Publishing/Graphics

CorelDRAW! Quick Reference	$ 8.95
Harvard Graphics Quick Reference	$ 8.95
Que's Using Ventura Publisher	$29.95
Using Animator	$24.95
Using DrawPerfect	$24.95
Using Harvard Graphics, 2nd Edition	$24.95
Using Freelance Plus	$24.95
Using PageMaker 4 for Windows	$29.95
Using PFS: First Publisher, 2nd Edition	$24.95
Using PowerPoint	$24.95
Using Publish It!	$24.95

Macintosh/Apple II

The Big Mac Book, 2nd Edition	$29.95
The Little Mac Book	$12.95
Que's Macintosh Multimedia Handbook	$24.95
Using AppleWorks, 3rd Edition	$24.95
Using Excel 3 for the Macintosh	$24.95
Using FileMaker	$24.95
Using MacDraw	$24.95
Using MacroMind Director	$29.95
Using MacWrite	$24.95
Using Microsoft Word 4: Macintosh Version	$24.95
Using Microsoft Works: Macintosh Version, 2nd Edition	$24.95
Using PageMaker: Macintosh Version, 2nd Edition	$24.95

Programming/Technical

C Programmer'sToolkit	$39.95
DOS Programmer's Reference, 2nd Edition	$29.95
Network Programming in C	$49.95
Oracle Programmer's Guide	$29.95
QuickC Programmer's Guide	$29.95
UNIX Programmer's Quick Reference	$ 8.95
UNIX Programmer's Reference	$29.95
UNIX Shell Commands Quick Reference	$ 8.95
Using Assembly Language, 2nd Edition	$29.95
Using BASIC	$24.95
Using Borland C++	$29.95
Using C	$29.95
Using QuickBASIC 4	$24.95
Using Turbo Pascal	$29.95

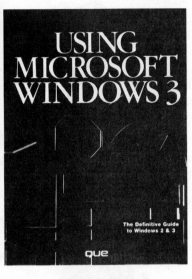